RIDE, RIDE, RIDE...

BY JOSIE RUSHO

Josie Rusho

CREDITS

Published by:	Outpost Books
	Kittitas, Washington
Printed and formatted by:	Abbott's Printing
	Yakima, Washington
Contributing writers:	Donna Evans, Donna Joncas,
	and Robin Owen
Cover design:	Josie Rusho and
	Abbott's Printing
Edited by:	Donna Evans
Front cover photo by:	Donna Joncas,
	Danville Georgetown
	Equestrian Park
Sketches, stories and maps by:	Josie Rusho

DISCLAIMER

"Ride, Ride, Ride..." is a trail-guide manual for horse enthusiasts. It is intended to direct you to horse trails and camps. Outpost Books is not liable for your actions or decisions. It's up to you to do the groundwork on the pathways you intend to visit by contacting resources, obtaining concise maps, verifying trail conditions, and checking weather forecasts. Take steps to ensure a chance for a successful trip, so you'll treasure your adventure into the beautiful Pacific Northwest. Make sure you and your mount are ready for the places you decide to explore. A ride on a well-conditioned horse or mule can be the most magnificent event you will ever experience. On the other hand, an unconditioned and mentally overloaded horse or mule can be a demanding affair to undergo. When picking a destination, consider the trail team's mind, body, and skill level. Be a selfless trail rider. Help a fellow rider along the trail whenever possible, so all concerned can claim a victory and continue to enjoy horse vacations. Above all, be safe and have fun.

ACKNOWLEDGEMENTS

My husband Cliff is my rock. I'll love you forever and ever. You're always there for me. You may not understand horses that well, but you understand me and that is what counts at the end of each day. Thanks to all of the new-found trail riders I get to travel with, and to the solid long-standing ones. You are matchless. I'd like to tip my hat to friends and fellow trail riders for sharing photos for this book. Pam Clemons graciously allowed me to use her photos of the mountain goats-thank you. I greatly appreciate the farriers (Paul and Rick) who put shoes on my horses. I would like to express thanks to Donna Evans, Robin Owen, and Donna Joncas, for being the contributing writers for this book. Donna Evans, I appreciate you for editing my book "Ride, Ride, Ride...". Abbott's Printing, you did a grand job again and it is my pleasure to work with you. The formatting, printing, and the little extras you do are treasured. I'm grateful to the diligent Forest Service, BLM, and Wilderness Rangers in Washington and Oregon for reviewing my manuscript for errors and upcoming trail changes. They include: The Ranger District of Fremont National Forest in Oregon; Silver Lake National Forest in Oregon; Crescent Ranger District in Oregon; Spokane BLM Outdoor Recreation Planner in Washington; and Crater Lake National Park in Oregon. I must mention my newest geldings, "Harley the palomino and Doc the dun". Welcome to the on-the-job-training. I am looking forward to more adventures upon your sturdy backs. To "Ali-Kat" my most cherished trail horse **EVER**! May you rest in peace. It was a delight to ride with you. Most of all, I'll always be indebted to the readers of my books. I hope to catch sight of you in camp or on the trail. I must say, it is great fun to meet you in the woods and share a campfire at camp. I like getting acquainted with your families, horses, mules, dogs, and having the opportunity to know you and to hear your stories.

Josie and Chief stop for a moment

Stormy waits at a trailhead

TABLE OF CONTENTS

Trails in Oregon State:

Trails in Washington State:

Indexes

Tim & Chief

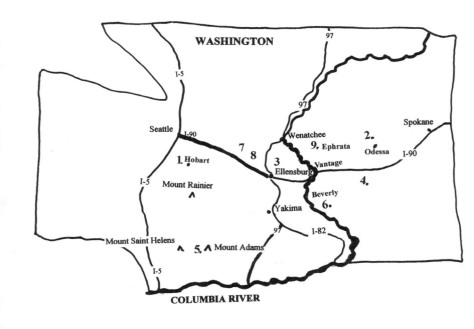

WASHINGTON

97

I-5

97

Seattle
I-90
7 8
Wenatchee
9. Ephrata
2.
Spokane
Odessa
I-90
1. Hobart
3
Ellensburg
Vantage
I-5
Mount Rainier
4.
∧
Beverly
6.
Yakima
Mount Saint Helens
97
I-82
I-5
5. ∧ Mount Adams

COLUMBIA RIVER

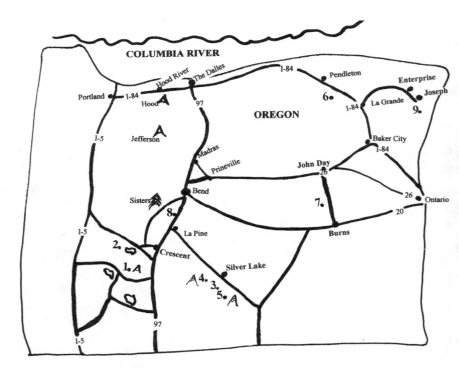

COLUMBIA RIVER

Hood River
The Dalles
I-84
Pendleton
Enterprise
Portland
I-84
Hood
∧
97
6.
I-84
La Grande
Joseph
9.
OREGON
I-5
Jefferson
∧
Baker City
I-84
Madras
Prineville
John Day
26
Sisters
Bend
7.
26
Ontario
8.
20
I-5
La Pine
Burns
2.
Crescent
1. A
Silver Lake
A 4.
3.
97
5. A
I-5

8

MAP OF OREGON AND WASHINGTON CAMP AND TRAILS

WASHINGTON

1. Danville Georgetown Equestrian Park
2. Lakeview Recreation Area
3. Naneum Ridge State Forest
4. Potholes Recreation Area
5. Cody Horse Camp
6. Crab Creek Wildlife
7. Coal Mines Trail
8. Jungle/Rye Creek Loop
9. Beezley Hills

Dean and Stormy

OREGON

1. Crater Lake, Diamond Lake, & Mount Thielsen Wilderness
2. Crescent Lake & Diamond Peak Wilderness
3. Silver Creek Marsh Horse Camp
4. Antler Trailhead Horse Camp
5. Farm Well Horse Camp
6. Meacham Emigrant Springs Horse Camp
7. Joaquin Miller Horse Camp
8. Todd Horse Camp
9. Eagle Cap Wilderness

OVERVIEW

Howdy, and welcome to another exploratory trip with me, your host Josie Rusho, and fellow riders: Donna Evans, Donna Joncas, and Robin Owen. We will guide you to places to ride your horses. The trails range from the low desert elevations to the highest mountain peaks in the Wilderness of Oregon and Washington States. There are so many places to see and

Cindy on Shelby in the medicine circle.

Josie & trail dog Daisy

discover in the Pacific Northwest. Pull on your boots and wave good-by to your T.V., computer and cell phones. Let's Ride, Ride, Ride. I've been to some grand new lands, and I can't wait to tell you about them. Come see lakes, rivers, mountains, scab-lands, and outback country. There are regions filled with views and memories just waiting to be experienced by you. The places we have visited have a lot to offer, so we dove in and came out with some real keepers. For some years now, I rode Forest Service trails almost exclusively. Recently, I've been riding some of the state lands, including some Bureau of Land Management areas (BLM). I used to think of these areas as reserved for fishermen and wildlife habitat stabilization, only focusing on them for late-fall and winter riding. Lately, my saddle pals and I have been camping in these regions in both the spring and the summertime, and we're pleased to pass our findings on to you. When I write about an area, first I do all of the homework. This includes conditioning my animals, finding a willing and able person (or group of people) that have the same riding goals as I do, and visiting the area. I focus hard on the facts and highlights of a region, taking the leg-work out of it, so you can have as carefree a trip as possible. I list the area's difficulty, elevations, horse facilities, and the mileage. I almost always give the experts of an area a chance to review my manuscripts so they can help with any changes or additional information. They add data they feel is warranted for me to pass along. Included in "Ride, Ride, Ride..." are maps and resource contacts for places to ride, as well as trails to access and, of course, the detailed directions to the camps and trailheads. I offer suggestions for camp food, fun and nearby places to eat and fill your tank. I think that a trip with your horse, mule, or pony is the best remedy for an overworked body and mind. Let's mark some time-out onto your calendar for you to play. You know you need it! The book is filled with pictures, sketches, and stories, with clear, concise, easy to read, no-nonsense knowledge. If you are looking for a certain place and don't see it in this book, perhaps it is in one of my other books: Gone Ridin', or Trail

Busters. To make trip memorabilia, consider having some tee-shirts made or silk scarves with embroidery done with the camp name and date, along with the names of the horses and riders. They make nice Christmas gifts. See you on the other side of the mountain. **Ride, Ride, Ride... your horse gently down the trail.**

AUTHOR'S STORY

I have been a resident of eastern Washington since 1986. I was born in Boulder, Colorado and have lived in Nevada and California. I've traveled a lot in Oregon and Idaho. I always wanted to ride my horse to make a living, so I can attest that dreams do come true. After all, somebody needs to do this job.

I have worked many jobs, starting when I was 12 years old weeding sapling trees. I have had the pleasure of milking cows, working at a butcher shop in a grocery store, and working for my dad in a machine shop. I took my turn at being a waitress, and in Las Vegas I was a car-hop at the world's largest dry cleaner. I've worked the front desk in a hotel and did the night audit. I have done other side-work with cattle, and raised and worked horses and cows. I am used to being outside. I always look for work that either includes outside jobs, or non-sedentary jobs. I am amazed that I ever wrote a book, much less that I am now on my 5th book. Thank God for spell-check and editors. The first two books were written with a co-author (out of print now). They are Grab Your Tails and Ride the Trails in 1997 and in

Sue on Willie, and Paul on Midnite riding near the Columbia River.

Brian and Echo riding in the high-desert.

2000 <u>Trail Blazing the Northwest</u>. I wrote my newest books <u>Gone Ridin'</u> in 2003 then <u>Trail Busters</u> in 2006. I now present to you <u>Ride, Ride, Ride...</u> .

My hobbies include hiking, snowshoeing, Jazzercise, and riding my horses.

A nice pastime that I enjoy in the spring is antler hunting (sheds). One of the best days is when you are riding and find an antler to bring home. I also love shopping for jeans, boots and cowboy shirts and an occasional cowboy hat. I wear the hat while riding until a low hung branch flings it off. I get too annoyed to stop and pick it up, so if you see my hat on the ground, you can have it, as it will not stay on my head!

It generally takes me 3-5 years to compile enough trails to produce a good, well-rounded book, with a variety of trails everyone would like

Donna E. and Andi.

to ride. I rely on input from fellow horse enthusiasts and word-of-mouth for new areas to canvas. By nature I'm snoopy and independent, so it is easy to find new spots to ride.

I married my sweetheart Cliff. He was the "boy next door". We have a son Nick, who I am extremely proud to say is serving our country in the United States Air Force. My horses Ali (RIP), Zephyr, Chief, Breezy, Harley, and Doc helped me write "Ride, Ride, Ride...". Some of the above have not worked out. One has passed on, one was hell on wheels, and one was stolen. But not to give up, I'm keeping the last two listed.

DEGREE OF TRAIL DIFFICULTY

The majority of trails in this book are rated "Moderate". The rating, to me, means that the trail is okay for the average, experienced rider and horse team. If there is anything on the trail that is potentially hazardous, it will be noted. I will either rate it "Challenging" or hyphenate the rating with the majority of the trail condition rated first. Example: "Moderate-Challenging" (bridge is broken-ford through deep mud) or "Challenging-Moderate" (majority of trail extremely steep). Few trails in Ride, Ride, Ride... are going to have just a "Challenging" rating. If they are, it means be extra careful. There are numerous possibilities for this rating. The reasons may be steepness, narrow conditions, late snow area with snow bridges and fields, or avalanche chutes. It may be jagged rocks, slide areas, unstable footing, deep swift water crossing, or a muddy bog. To find out why, just read the trail description. Be safe and when in doubt "Don't do it". Most trail riders are not out to prove anything to anyone or to show-off. Just have fun, use common sense, and take home great memories.

CONSIDERATION FOR THE FOREST

The Forest Service, Bureau of Land Management and other stewards of the forest, desert and protected lands want you to take care of designated recreational areas, so we can all enjoy them forever and ever. You can do your part by obeying all of the rules posted, keeping gates shut and cleaning up after yourselves. This ensures our next generation will have the same freedom to roam and explore this great country of ours. In camp, clean up all horse manure and keep horses away from water sources when tied. Use your "horse sense". It will go a long way in helping to keep the regions open to horse enthusiasts. Pack out all trash. Put out all fires-cool to the touch.

Dean and Stormy ride in the snow.

FAREWELL TO THE FINEST

Madeleine Bratt and her mare Falinka

She lived a full life and will be missed by all who knew her. We rode our mares together on some hard trails. Madeleine and I climbed high ridges upon their strong backs, and depended on their sure-footedness to ford swift streams and traverse narrow

Madeleine and Falinka

tread. And always, always after our rides together, we filled our bellies and recalled the day in the saddle, as we watched the glowing embers of our campfire soften. With deep sadness and fond memories, I bid you

farewell. I learned a lot from you. "A great life is not measured by the number of breaths taken, but by the number of moments that have taken your breath away." Madeleine died suddenly in 2007 of natural causes. Her mare passed separately in 2007 as well.

Ali-Kat and her un-born foal

She was the most athletic, quickest, and most intelligent horse I've ever had the pleasure to call my own. The unexpected complications of pregnancy took her in March 2008, and the unborn buckskin filly was lost on Feb. 29, 2008 (leap year). I'm not sure you ever get over this kind of loss. Ali put up a long 3 week fight for her life. Sadly, she lost the struggle, as her organs started failing. I thank W.S.U. for their efforts to save my precious mare, and for making her comfortable in her last days.

Josie and Ali

Crater Lake Pepper Poppers

- ❖ 12 jalapeño peppers or an assortment of small hot red, green and yellow peppers
- ❖ 1 pair latex type of gloves (be sure put on your hands before handling peppers!)
- ❖ 1 ½ cup of soft cream cheese
- ❖ Hot sauce to taste
- ❖ Dry chili pepper seeds and or chili powder to taste
- ❖ ¼ cup of bacon (pre-cooked)
- ❖ 1 cup flour or enough to dredge with
- ❖ 3 eggs
- ❖ ¼ cup of milk
- ❖ 2 cups of seasoned bread crumbs or cracker crumbs seasoned to taste
- ❖ Olive oil

Cut the peppers in half and top off the stems. Then clean out the seeds and white pulp, rinse and drain, set aside. Be sure to use some latex gloves on your hands to prevent the hot juice from burning. In a bowl, make a filling using the cream cheese, hot sauce, dry chili pepper seeds and or chili powder. Mix in the cooked bacon pieces. Fill the peppers with the cream cheese mixture. Set up three bowls: one with flour, one with whipped egg and milk wash, and the last with crunched up crackers or bread crumbs. First, dredge your peppers in flour, then in the egg wash, and lastly-roll them in the bread crumbs. Bake these little hotty's on a cookie sheet wiped with olive oil. Place them onto the sheet and drip olive oil sparingly on top of poppers. Bake at 350 degrees for 25 minutes. Broil for 3 minutes for that golden-brown touch. I like to make these ahead of time. Cut them up on top of a salad or into an egg omelet. They are good by themselves, with or without a dip. Ranch dressing works good. Crater Lake Pepper Poppers can be cooked over a campfire in a heavy pan.

Yummy.

Pot Holes Flappers

- 3 cups grated cheese
- 2 tablespoons flour
- 1 egg
- 1 bunch cilantro
- 3 celery stalks
- 1 small onion
- Oil
- Sour cream to taste

Grind vegetables to a pulp in a bowl and set aside. Mix cheese and flour in another bowl. Heat a non-stick skillet with a little oil on medium heat. Take a large pinch of cheese-covered flour and lay 4 separate mounds into pan. With the back of a spoon flatten the mounds out like a pancake. Spoon a layer of vegetable pulp on top of cheese, then again cheese on top of the vegetable mix. Cook, as undisturbed as possible until you can lift the flappers. Flip them onto the other side. They should be golden brown. Top with a dollop of sour cream. You can successfully pulp your vegetables at home in a food processor. Store the pulp in a zipper bag. This makes it very convenient to cook in camp. This makes enough for two people-about six flappers.

Bannocks

You can add or subtract to these recipes. It's an ancient staple believed to come from the Scot's. It uses oat flour, which is the same ingredient given to their horses who where strong and known for endurance. Mountain men and the first explorers of the new world are said to have passed on this information. Bannock is high in carbohydrates and a wonderful primary food. In conjunction with proteins, it can be used as a complete meal. You may add different combinations of wild foraged edibles such as meat, fish and fruits. Some have added cheese or nuts as well as seeds. The sky is the limit. Wilderness trappers, and prospectors, as well as soldiers and explorers all have legendary tales about this great survival food-simple dough wrapped

around a stick and cooked. Bannock has been known as: bush bread, trail bread, grease bread and galette, but we call it plain ol' good! These recipes and the history were found on the web. For more information, go to "http:/www.survivaltopics.com/ survival/bannock/">Bannock</ a> I hope you give these a go. I like to cook a hot dog in the middle of my Bannock.

Josie and Harley, Donna J. and Penny.

Outback multi-flour Bannock

- ❖ 1 cup barley flour
- ❖ 1 cup wheat flour
- ❖ ½ cup rolled oats
- ❖ 1 cup sugar
- ❖ ½ to 1 cup raisins or other dried fruits
- ❖ 1 ½ cup buttermilk
- ❖ 1 teaspoon baking powder
- ❖ 1 tablespoon coarse ground salt
- ❖ 1 tablespoon cinnamon
- ❖ 1 tablespoon cloves
- ❖ 1 tablespoon nutmeg
- ❖ Enough water to make a dough ball

This is a fruity and spice-filled belly-pleaser. Mix together all ingredients and make a ball of dough and then flatten it to be about ½ inch thick in the shape of a bread stick-however, tapered at each end. Take a green stick and wrap the dough around it and slowly roast the Bannock over a hot fire, rotating periodically until it turns a golden brown. You can also cook to form a loaf shape in a Dutch oven. This is a hearty, rib-sticking meal.

Outback fried Bannocks

- ❖ 4 cups flour
- ❖ 2 tablespoons baking powder
- ❖ 2 tablespoons sugar
- ❖ ½ cup milk
- ❖ ¼ cup butter (½ stick)
- ❖ 2 eggs
- ❖ ¼ tablespoon salt
- ❖ Oil for frying

Mix into a ball of dough, then break off pieces and flatten into rounds about ½ inch thick. Fry in a pan of oil until golden brown. Serve with other food or eat it by itself. It is sure satisfying after a long wonderful ride in the forest. Feel free to dip in jelly or coat with syrup-use your imagination.

Cindy and Rocky crossing a high desert stream.

Marie's Camp Muffins

Serves as many as you make!

- ❖ 1 egg
- ❖ Several slices of cooked ham or Canadian Bacon
- ❖ 1 English Muffin
- ❖ 1 slice of Cheddar Cheese

Fry eggs hard. After turning egg over, place warmed ham or bacon on top, then the cheese. Heat until cheese is melted. Toast and butter English Muffin and put egg inside. Sit by the fire and enjoy!

Mount Adams Huckleberry-Stuffed French Toast

Serves 3

- ❖ 6 slices of homemade buttermilk egg-bread (see recipe below)
- ❖ 4 eggs
- ❖ ½ cup heavy cream
- ❖ ½ teaspoon cinnamon
- ❖ ½ teaspoon vanilla
- ❖ 2 tablespoons of sugar
- ❖ ¼ teaspoon of salt
- ❖ 5 ounces of Huckleberry jam
- ❖ 8 ounces of whipped cream cheese (whip your own or buy it pre-whipped)
- ❖ 2-4 Tablespoons of butter for the frying pan
- ❖ 2 ½ cups of cornflake crumbs (crush your own or buy in a box)

Cut the bread into 6 medium thick slices (about ½ inch thick). On three halves you will spread Huckleberry jam and on the other three halves you will dollop a big spoonful of whipped cream cheese. Close them up into 3 sandwiches. In 2 flat bowls, or small pans, place the cornflake crumbs in one and in the other, beat eggs, cream, spices, and salt. Take one sandwich at a time and gently soak all sides in the egg mixture and then roll in the crumbs. In a medium hot skillet put butter and melt until hot. Place sandwiches into skillet and cook on medium heat until golden brown. Leave as undisturbed as possible-flip and cook other side. Finish up by holding up the edges, one side at a time, in the butter to cook. When done: plate and eat. There is no need for syrup. These are crunchy on the outside and creamy-dreamy on the inside. Just what a trail-rider needs to hold them over until lunch.

Homemade Buttermilk Egg-Bread

1 ½ pound loaf made in a bread machine at home:
- ❖ 2 eggs (room temperature is best)
- ❖ 2/3 cup of buttermilk (90-100 degrees)
- ❖ 3 cups of white flour
- ❖ 1 ½ teaspoons of salt
- ❖ 2 ½ tablespoons of sugar
- ❖ 1 ½ tablespoons butter
- ❖ 2 teaspoons of active or bread machine fast rise yeast

As with all bread machine mixes, put the wet ingredients in the bottom of the pan, then flour, salt, and sugar. Separate the butter into 4 equal parts and put one part into each edge of the pan. Make a dent in the center of the pan and put the yeast in. Turn on the machine and in about 3 hours you have great bread for the French Toast (see above recipe). Make a day ahead of time before you leave on your horse camping trip.

Naneum Ridge broiled ginger-vanilla grapefruit

Serves 6
- ❖ 6 grapefruit-sliced crosswise and sectioned
- ❖ 2/3 cup of sugar
- ❖ 3 teaspoons ginger (powered or fresh grated crystallized)
- ❖ ¾ teaspoon vanilla bean crushed into a powder (whole or just the bean)

Prepare at home,-grind sugar, ginger, and vanilla bean. Place cut grapefruit (meat side up) onto a pan (cookie sheet works well), top with sugar mix and broil till hot and tops are brown. I think you could do this in a dutch oven too. This is the most delicious way I have ever eaten grapefruit. Give it a whirl. You can make this at home and eat it cold at camp.

Mountain Lake Sausage and Egg Roll-up

Serves 4 (or 2 very hungry trail riders)
- ❖ 4 eggs (hardboiled)
- ❖ ¾ pound breakfast sausage
- ❖ 1 hot skillet
- ❖ 4 hardy appetites

Make 4 patties of sausage, about 3 inches wide (depends on how big your egg is). Place a hardboiled egg in the center of the sausage and wrap it around, pinch it together and smooth it out making it seamless. Place into a medium hot skillet and roll as it cooks. Be sure to cook all sides nice and brown. Mountain Lake Sausage and Egg Roll-up make a great side-dish with pancakes, or eat it alone with some steaming hot coffee. Enjoy your vacation time while you sit by a mountain lake and savor this breakfast. You can hard-boil the eggs ahead of time.

Donna's Zippy Omelet-it is a power-breakfast

Serve 1 dose for every trail rider, to start their day right.
- ❖ 2 eggs
- ❖ Milk (optional)
- ❖ Ham or Bacon
- ❖ cut vegetables-onions & green pepper
- ❖ 1 slice of cheddar cheese
- ❖ Salsa
- ❖ Salt and pepper
- ❖ Zip-bag (quart size)

Open the bag and put in all ingredients and shake up until mixed well. Burp air out of bag and zip shut. Slide bag into boiling water and let cook for 13-15 min. until done. Your omelet will come out in one nice piece, ready to eat! Try it, you'll like it. Consider having some fruit and or sweet rolls to go along-side to make a tasty breakfast.

Saddle Tramp Soda

Serves 1
- ❖ 1 Root Beer soda
- ❖ ¼ cup of half and half
- ❖ Spray of whipped cream

Mix soda and half and half. Top with a good solid squirt of whipped cream. The canned type works well.

Irish Soda

Serves 1
- ❖ 1 can of Root Beer
- ❖ ¼ cup of Irish Cream Liquor
- ❖ 1 spurt of whipped cream

Take the root beer, add Irish Cream and top with whipped cream.

> *I dedicate this book to my friend Terri, for all of the grand years of riding together on the trails.*

CRATER LAKE, DIAMOND LAKE & MOUNT THIELSEN WILDERNESS
(Crater Lake Horse Camp)

Crater Lake, Diamond Lake and Mount Thielsen Wilderness are situated in south central Oregon and provide fabulous riding opportunities. These areas are being kept pristine and clean with hard work from the different agency personnel, non-profit youth organizations and visitors alike. Upon seeing the natural beauty of the surroundings and the nice facilities provided you'll be glad to be a steward of the region as well. I'm sure we all want these priceless spots to stay open forever. There is a primitive horse camp with trails leading out of it, along with several outlying trailheads nearby that you can trailer to, keeping you occupied for a week or so. Most days you can plan on riding the main trail through the area which is the Pacific Crest National Scenic Trail (PCT) #2000 (it travels north and south from Canada to Mexico). I will describe one loop ride meandering down from the horse camp to the tranquil Diamond Lake and back up using a mixed bag of trails including a small section of the PCT #2000. Diamond Lake is 10,000 years old. It was named for John Diamond in 1849. The lake is 2,824 acres, 52 feet deep, 1.5 miles wide, 3.5 miles long, and is 11.2 miles around. Water and fuel are available at Diamond Lake Resort. There are 3 restaurants, and a lodge built in 1923. A ride going north from camp on the PCT #2000 takes you into the Mount Thielsen Wilderness. Mount Thielsen stands at 9182'. It is a peak with a unique splendor all its own. The rides in this chapter are in the moderate-difficulty range and the footing is sandy with very few rocks. To gain access to ride inside Crater Lake National Park be advised there are only two trailheads which you are allowed to park a horse trailer at within Crater Lake National Park. One is at the southern end, and the other is at the northern end. At the northern

Camp dogs; Bo, puppy Daisy, and Pepper

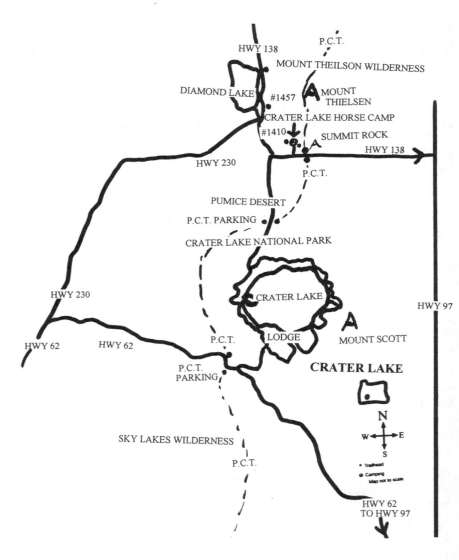

trailhead you must pay a day fee to enter the park. The southern trailhead is outside the fee area on the main road before you turn in to the main attraction area. Please obey all regulations pertaining to stock travel and stay on the trails designated for horses. A friend and I set a day aside to treat ourselves to the sights, giving the horses a day off, so we began by going down to eat breakfast at Diamond Lake Resort. We admired the beauty of the lake, Mount Bailey and the boats. Then we drove around to the southern entrance of the park and visited the renowned Crater Lake where we toured Crater Lake Lodge, milled around the gift shop for souvenirs, got a coffee, some lunch, and then strolled to Sinnott Memorial Overlook. This is the most fabulous lake I have ever seen in my life. The blue color is deeper than you could ever imagine and the outlying rim of the immense crater and Phantom Ship Island are all absolutely breathtaking. We drove the Rim Drive Road which goes around the lake, and through the park where you come out almost exactly at the horse camp by the north entrance. There are lots of spots along the narrow winding road to stop and gawk at the magnificent Crater Lake. The lake is 1,943 feet deep, 6 miles wide and is at 6173' elevation. The highest point of the rim is 8151' and the highest point in the park is Mount Scott at 8929'. The average snowfall is 44 feet and it gets an average of 66 inches of precipitation a year. When you visit, you will learn a lot about the lake's facts and figures. Be sure to stop over on a clear day and remember your camera. We also took a video camera. Crater Lake is not visible from the designated horse trails so this made a fun outing and we took home lots of great memories. There is a daily fee to enter the park near the lake from either entrance. I would **not** recommend driving your truck and trailer through the park any further than to get from camp to the northern trailhead, so unhook for a nice day drive. The rim road is narrow with blind curves and is extremely popular, (you can go during the week and avoid the main throng of visitors). When we wanted to ride from the south end we took our trailers around to access

The stunningly beautiful Crater lake

the southern trailhead instead of trying to go through the park. There is gasoline and water at the camper store at Mazama Village, which is inside the park at the southern end.

*Notes: The Crater Lake National Park staff and trail supervisor wish trail riders to know that the Bald Crater Loop Trail is also an option to ride although it wasn't ridden on my excursion. They said that it is **not** highly recommended as it is often the last area to receive trail clearing and more than half the trail is on a 2 to 3 year clearing rotation. Horse users also are not allowed into the Boundary Springs (2 miles from loop) or Crater Springs (¼ mile from Loop) areas. It mainly is a ride through forested areas similar to other closer trails. It would be approximately 22 miles from the northern Pacific Crest Trailhead. They also said that they have completed additional improvements on the Pacific Crest Trail #2000 since I visited.

Directions to Crater Lake Horse Camp: The horse camp is on the north side of Crater Lake off paved Highway138 to the east of Diamond Lake. The mileage from Bend is about 85 miles, Medford 87 miles, Klamath Falls 75 miles, Chemult 77 miles, and Roseburg 82 miles. If coming in from the east or south you'll come in on Highway 138 from Highway 97 (there are two turnoffs to Crater Lake from Highway 97, one going to the northern entrance and another to the southern. Both are well signed, but use the northern one taking Highway 138 west to reach camp). If coming in from the southwest you'll come in on Highway 230 from Highway 62, and if coming in from I-5 or Roseburg from the west use Highway 138 going east. The sign off Highway 138 reads "North Crater Lake Trailhead". Turn here, then after driving down a little ways the sign reads "Crater Lake Horse Camp". Camp is at 5900' so you may want to acclimate yourself and your mount for a day or so before riding very hard if you are coming from a low altitude. The gravel road in to camp is narrow with turnouts and is about ½ mile or so long.

Crater Lake Horse Camp includes: Crater Lake Horse Camp is a small trailhead camp and is primitive. There is a miniature loop at the end of the road in to camp. Amenities include a vault toilet, 3 hitching rails, 3 camp sites that are the walk-in type, some tables, fire pits, loading ramp and there is garbage service. The down side is that there is **no water at all** so you need to bring your own and refill where you can. We found Diamond Lake Resort to have what we needed. You'll need a Forest Service Pass to park, but no other fee is required. There is quite a bit of room if the hikers' cars are parked considerately. We came in on a Sunday and had no problem getting settled.

For more information contact:

Crater Lake National Park
P.O. Box 7
Crater Lake, OR 97604-0007
541-594-3000
www.nps.gov/crla

Maps to use:
National Park Service- Crater Lake Map
Oregon Road & Recreation Atlas
Mount Thielsen Wilderness
(Sky Lakes Wilderness is somewhat helpful as well)

Sign on the Pacific Crest Trail.   *Crusty lava on Crater Lake's rim.*

Crater Lake #1410

Distance: 8 Miles
Altitude: 5183'-5920'
Map: Mount Thielsen Wilderness
Difficulty: Moderate

Directions: Crater Lake Trail #1410 begins from Crater Lake Horse Camp by the vault toilet. It is well signed.

Connecting Trails: 2000, Diamond Lake Loop, 1457, 1448, and 1458

Horse Camping: Crater Lake Horse Camp

Trail Description: Crater Lake Trail #1410 goes two ways from Crater Lake Horse Camp. The trail to the east is all timberland with sandy footing and connects to the PCT #2000 in ½ mile. The wooded trail to the west turns into a small 2-track road in about 1 mile. Cross a small dirt road where Crater Lake Trail #1410 becomes a single trail again. Travel down a draw to intersect with Diamond Lake Loop Trail at the 3 mile-point. Watch for blue diamond markers in the trees guiding you along Crater Lake Trail #1410. There are markers tacked to the trees indicating the mileage. Occasionally you'll see a sign with the trail name and mileage. The foliage from camp to the first paved road is somewhat arid. However, after you cross the road, you are in deep woods. Then you will cross another paved road into deeper timberland with meadows. One more road to cross, (this time it is dirt) which will be your return route on the way back if you choose to make a loop (Summit Rock Trail #1457). We noticed funny little markers and arrows on the ground along this stretch. Ride behind houses and an RV area. There is a view of Mount Thielsen on the right. Next you'll see Diamond Lake's east shoreline. This section from here to the end has wooden park-like benches, just sitting in the woods! Ford a small creek, still in forest, then you'll cross another stream. This one has a foot bridge-too wobbly for horses. We encountered a nice meadow but it was too bad that it had hidden smooth wire underfoot in the grass. Our mounts got tangled but kept their heads and were fine. We had stopped for lunch and had gotten off trail. Cross a small dirt road with snowmobile signs. Crater Lake Trail #1410 becomes a small road, and everything is well signed. Your horses may be alerted by spewing water coming out of a pipe onto rocks beside the trail since it is very noisy. Watch for a semi-hidden fence line with woven wire lying on the ground near the trail. The trail ends at a horse corral, which is also a trailhead for two other trails, #1448 and #1458.

*Note: Some signs read "N. CRATER TR. 1410" and others read "Crater Lake 1410".

Gnarly trees on the PCT #2000 near Crater Lake

Lightning Springs

Distance: 4 Miles
Altitude: 5900'-8001'
Map: Mount Thielsen Wilderness
Difficulty: Moderate

Directions: Lightning Springs Trail begins from PCT #2000 about 1 mile south of Bybee Creek Stock Camp.

Connecting Trail: 2000

Horse Camping: Bybee Creek Stock Camp if you like to pack-in

Trail Description: This brief outline for Lightning Springs Trail is written by the Crater Lake Staff. The trail supervisor and staff were kind enough to review my manuscript for the Crater Lake National Park chapter of this book. Here is what they have to say for this trail.

"Horses are allowed on the Lightning Springs Trail to within a ¼ mile of the caldera rim. Horse users will find two hitching posts for their use. They can hike the last ¼ mile to view Crater Lake. It is a steady 4.5 mile climb to the rim. The trail follows an old fire road so the grades are not steep. The trail travels through Lodgepole pine forests to larger Mountain Hemlocks and Shasta Red Fir forests in the upper half. There also are several pumice fields and a few mountain streams found in the upper half. The fire seen on the PCT also traveled through this area."

Diamond Lake, view from the Mount Thielsen Wilderness on the PCT

Josie & Ali at the gateway to Mt. Thielsen Wilderness

Pacific Crest Trail #2000

(From camp ride north to Mount Thielsen)

Distance: 4.5 Miles	
Altitude: 5925'-8000'	
Map: Mount Thielsen Wilderness	
Difficulty: Moderate	

Directions: From Crater Lake Horse Camp ride Crater Lake Trail #1410 west for ½ mile to the "T" intersection with the Pacific National Scenic Trail #2000. Turn north (left).

Connecting Trails: 1410 and 1457

Horse Camping: Crater Lake Horse Camp

Trail Description: Begin the ascent toward Mount Thielsen on the PCT #2000. The forest is sparse and the trail is wide and smooth. Ride about ½ mile to a road which is Summit Rock Trail #1457. Cross over it and continue on. There are signs to guide you along to your destination. Soon you'll be in the Mount Theilsen Wilderness marked by a sign in the trees. Usually you will see a sign-in box when entering a Wilderness, however none exists here. It is a gradual climb with a couple of switchbacks which are hardly noticeable. Here the trail curves to the east side of a hill and around to the north. You'll observe views of Crater Lake to the south and Diamond Lake below to the west. The trail makes a horseshoe shape around the next mountain. Here you will get up-close-and-personal with jaggy Mount Thielsen standing at a whopping 9182' tall. The peak seemed significantly bigger than I thought it would, maybe because we snuck up on it in the cold shadow of the mountain with the wind whipping our faces. The tread becomes a bit narrower here but is still good. There is a rock slide area ahead and open areas. We turned back at this point as our goal was to go for a stretch, not an all day excursion. We returned to where there was enough room to sit on the warmer, sunny side of the hill and enjoy the wanderlust views of Diamond Lake below. Word has it that beyond the rock slide the trail becomes narrower. We enjoyed our highland trip into Mount Thielsen Wilderness. From camp, this makes a short 10 mile outing and is intermittently in forest.

Pacific Crest Trail #2000

(From camp ride south to Crater Lake National Park's north trailhead)

Distance: 7 Miles
Altitude: 5925'-6500'
Maps: Mount Thielsen Wilderness and Crater Lake National Park
Difficulty: Moderate

Directions: From Crater Lake Horse Camp ride Crater Lake Trail #1410 west for ½ mile to the "T" intersection with the Pacific National Scenic Trail #2000. Turn south (right).

Connecting Trails: 1410 and a hikers-only trail near Grouse Hill

Horse Camping: Crater Lake Horse Camp

Trail Description: Go south on the Pacific Crest National Scenic Trail #2000. Soon you'll cross Highway 138. The forest is first thick and then thins out with more grass areas along the way. Notice the weird knobby and gnarled trees. The forest becomes denser with big trees and less grass. The first 4 miles goes slightly uphill then back down for a ways. The trail becomes level and more parched, and then downhill some more onto remnants of an old road. There are a number of rocks along-side the trail. However the trail itself is not rocky. You'll skirt an exposed area that is flat on the right-hand side of the path. This area is called Pumice Desert (collecting rocks is prohibited). There is a view of Mount Thielsen and you'll find a trail box for registration and information. The trail goes back in to a meager forest with a slight incline. You'll make your way along the boulder laden Grouse Hill which stands at 7412'. Intersect with a "hiker only" trail leaving going south (left). The PCT #2000 veers to the right to cross the park's north entrance road, which is paved. On the other side of the road is a trailhead for horse trailer rigs as well as hikers' vehicles. There is NO WATER along this section of the PCT #2000. I would suggest bringing some extra water in your saddle bags and a small collapsible dish to pour water into for your horse to drink. It helps curb the thirst of your mount (dog dishes work great!). From camp and back this is a 15 mile ride.

Pacific Crest Trail #2000

(From Crater Lake National Park's north trailhead ride south to Bybee Creek Stock Camp)

Distance: 9.6 Miles	
Altitude: 5900'-6200'	
Maps: Mount Thielsen Wilderness and Crater Lake	
Difficulty: Moderate	

Directions: From Highway 138 drive into the north entrance to Crater Lake Park. It is well signed. You will be required to pay a day fee to enter, which was $10.00 when we visited. Drive 7 miles to the north trailhead which is on the right-hand side of the road, and is rather small. Getting there early is my advice. There is room for large rigs to make the circle in the parking area but the trick is if there is enough room to park.

Connecting Trails: Bald Crater and Sphagnum Bog

Horse Camping: Nearby, Crater Lake Horse Camp and if you are packing-in use Bybee Creek Stock Camp

OLD FRIENDS & FAVORITE HORSES

Old friends may throw in the towel,
Your favorite horse may die,
Become the coyote and give a howl,
Sit for awhile and sigh!
When you feel you are all done,
Dust off your be-hind,
 Now is the time for having fun,
Letting the shadows fall behind,
The past is over, face to the sun!

Trail Description: I will describe this trail starting from the northern trailhead in the Crater Lake National Park. Ride your horse following the PCT #2000 going south toward Bybee Creek Stock Camp. It is a forested area interrupted briefly by a small tip of pumice desert. You'll see the beautiful Red Cone. The trail is an over grown road through the length of this 9.6 mile stretch to Bybee Creek Stock Camp. The path rolls along and skirts the west side of Red Cone. The PCT #2000 travels into deeper forest with small meadows. The footing is pretty sandy and has small stones here and there. You'll see the trail to Bald Crater leaving to the right. For the next 1.5 miles in a somewhat shady portion of the trek you'll go upward a bit into an area with bigger trees. There is no grass at all and the footing is sandy. Go further around a knoll and the trail flattens through lush meadows and springs. You'll see the turnoff for Sphagnum Bog Trail which goes the same way as the last one. (Both of these trails are open to stock and can be used in creating a loop). The springs are noticeable if you recognize the wetland type of grass growing along the trail. The path descends slightly along this damper section with tall, sumptuous grass. There is a creek, and then another stream with a culvert. Come into a burn area which at first is only on the left side of the PCT #2000. Before you know it, you will see the small wooden sign marking Bybee Creek and the trail into its stock camp. Read the next section to find out how to get to Bybee Creek Stock Camp from the south end of the park.

Josie stretches out at lunch-time.

Pacific Crest Trail #2000

(From Crater Lakes Park's south trailhead ride north to
Bybee Creek Stock Camp)

Distance: 7.3 Miles	
Altitude: 5900'-6200'	
Maps: Mount Thielsen Wilderness and Crater Lake	
Difficulty: Moderate	

Directions: From Highway 62, drive in to the roadside trailhead (not in the fee area). The trailhead is nice and big enough for any size rig. Get there early for easy parking. No vault toilet or other facilities are found at this trailhead.

Connecting Trails: Dutton Creek (hikers only) and Lightning Spring

Horse Camping: Nearby, Crater Lake Horse Camp and if you are packing-in, use Bybee Creek Stock Camp. Driving from Crater Lake Horse Camp, it is a ways around to this trailhead, so I suggest going out to eat at the cafe on Highway 97. Or if coming in from the west go to Diamond Lake to eat. Hey, you're on vacation for Pete's sake!

Trail Description: This section of the PCT #2000 will be described from the southern trailhead at Crater Lake National Park and will go north for about 7.3 miles to reach Bybee Creek Stock Camp. Start by crossing paved Highway 62 and entering forest. At first it is flat, and then climbs to a rocky area. Next it levels then goes over a hump and down a hillside slope. With the use of one switchback it takes you to a smooth grassland area. There is a little bit of rocks along this piece. The trail goes into a burn area with various spots being more charred than others. You'll have a view of the surrounding hills and will meet with a multitude of streams. The burn is one-sided at times. The trail is rolling and the green grass and black trunks make an eerie contrast. There are new-looking wooden water-bars placed intermittently on the trail to help curb erosion of the soil. The terrain is interesting with rock knolls. The creeks are cool and clear and easy to ford, providing a liquid type of "water bar" for the horses to drink from. You'll pass Dutton Creek Trail (hikers only). Quite a ways closer to Bybee Creek is another trail turnoff for Lightning Spring. Overall the trail is nice with only a few areas of rock. One section that we found fascinating had a wonderful Halloween look to it with orange needles littering on the forest floor and black charred remains of old trees left clinging to sterile ground. The PCT #2000 heads downward to meet up with Bybee Creek and a wooden sign directing you to Bybee Creek Stock Camp.

*Note: The Crater Lake Staff suggests a ride I did not get a chance to do while I visited Crater Lake National Park. It starts from this trailhead and goes south to Stuart Falls (approximately 16 miles round trip). Stuart Falls Trail is a newer reroute which provides some wonderful views of the Sky Lakes Wilderness. The falls actually lie within the Sky Lakes Wilderness boundary which has even more riding options.

Who, who, who would do a thing like that?   *Bald eagle in flight at Josie's house.*

Mount Thielsen

Summit Rock #1457

Distance: 4.5 Miles	
Altitude: 5183'- 6000'	
Map: Mount Thielsen Wilderness	
Difficulty: Moderate	

Directions: There is no real trailhead for this trail. East end: use the PCT #2000 near Mount Thielsen about 1 mile north from camp or to gain access. West end: use the Crater Lake Trail #1410 near Diamond Lake to gain access.

Connecting Trails: 2000 and 1410

Horse Camping: Close by Crater Lake Horse Camp

Trail Description: Summit Rock Trail #1457 is a dirt road and it connects Crater Lake Trail #1410 near Diamond Lake to the Pacific Crest Trail #2000 near Mount Thielsen. It is a wonderful sandy road with forest lining it all the way. From the Diamond Lake area it climbs nearly 1000' on a gentle slope. From Crater Lake Trail #1410 (near Diamond Lake) go east on this trail. It crosses a paved road, and on the other side of the road you'll find your way marked with an orange sign reading Summit Rock 7 miles. It is only about 4 ½ miles to the PCT #2000. This is not the most interesting ride but, hey, it helps make a loop! (We explored a little and found another option to return to camp: use the Summit Rock Trail #1457 from Diamond Lake and go 4 miles or so. Turn right when you see a sign that reads: "Crater Lake" and travel on an old overgrown road. You may need to go up and over or around several downed trees, but ride about ½ mile to where Crater Lake Trail #1410 crosses over. You'll recognize the blue diamond markings: turn right and go back to camp.)

CRESCENT LAKE & DIAMOND PEAK WILDERNESS
(Whitefish Horse Camp)

Crescent Lake and Diamond Peak Wilderness are located in south central Oregon. Views across Crescent Lake and from the entire area include Diamond Peaks 7068', Lakeview Mountain 7066', Redtop Mountain 6948' and an assortment of buttes and unnamed mountains. My riding partner and I thought that the south and west part of this area beyond Crescent Lake and up by Summit Lake were as wild and beautiful as the Diamond Peak Wilderness. The Whitefish Horse Camp is a lolly-pop shaped camp and sits under nice trees. Across the main road is the immense Crescent Lake with its little island and wonderful beach. Leave the horse at camp and come on over for a swim, walk, or just sit and ponder the views of the buttes and other mountains in the area. My friend and I took our mountain bikes and rode around the whole area on our day off. There is a resort where you can get a hot shower for a minimal fee or go for dinner out. There is a gas station a short ways away and a small store. The Diamond Peak Wilderness covers 52,737 acres. Diamond Peak is 8744' and is the most prominent landmark in the Wilderness. In July of 1852, John Diamond and William Macy climbed what is now Diamond Peak. A month later, they returned

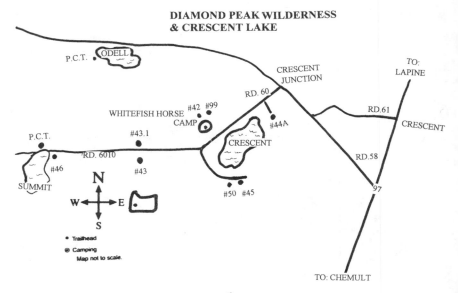

DIAMOND PEAK WILDERNESS
& CRESCENT LAKE

with 5 others, looking for a pathway for a wagon route over the Cascade Mountain Range. They found a way over what is now called Emigrant Pass. As with a large number of land formations in Oregon, Diamond Peak is a remnant of a massive volcano which has been sectioned into 4 individual peaks by ice age glacier activity along the Cascade Crest. This one goes north and south as well as having ridges that expand towards the east and west. At the 7200' level and up you'll find that bulky lava, pumice, and rusty color cinders make up the open sloped terrain. Above timberline, stubby whitebark pines dig in their roots and cling to life. Views in the Wilderness and surrounding area include; Mount Yoran, Lakeview and Redtop Mountains, as well as Maiden Peak further to the northeast. All of these are also volcanic in structure. The lower elevation is treed, mostly with mountain hemlock and true firs. The eastern section has large stands of lodgepole pine trees. This land has many flowers and grasses including beargrass, lupine, and heather and is sprinkled with huckleberry bushes as well. They line your trails and meadows, and the shorelines of streams and lakes. Lakes are plentiful in the Diamond Peak Wilderness and adjacent to it also. One of the best views of the Diamond Peaks is from Diamond View Lake. You'll take Whitefish Creek Trail #42 from camp to reach this "Must See" destination. Wildlife includes black bears, black-tailed deer, mule deer, elk, pine martens, squirrels, snowshoe rabbits, pikas, marmots

Whitefish Horse Camp

and foxes. Some inhabit the area, and some visit seasonally. Birds of a feather are: Clark's Nutcracker, raven, grey jays, Bald Eagles, Great Grey Owls, Ospreys and water ouzel which haunt the Wilderness area. Around the lakes, keep an eye peeled for nesting Goldeneye and Bufflehead ducks. The Pacific Crest National Scenic Trail #2000 has a stretch of 16 miles in the Diamond Peak Wilderness and leaves to the north going towards Waldo Lake Wilderness. Expect snow fields until August. There are close to 60 miles of trails (mileage calculated one-way as always!) to explore on horseback in the Wilderness and another 30 miles outside of the Wilderness to the south. The trails are excellent for horseback riding and are in the moderate category. There are many lakes ranging from deep green to icy blue, and rocky shorelines to sandy beaches. All having their own magic charm enticing you to set a spell. Whitefish Horse Camp is a busy place so make your calls ahead of time to be sure to get the dates you want. We went after Labor Day and it was still a bustling place. Be sure to call ahead to see when the water will be turned off and if the manure disposal service is still available as well as if a fee is being charged. If you plan to visit after Labor Day you may want to add an extra day or two in case the weather gets gnarly and wet or maybe even snowy. If the weather turns, it is much nicer to spend the extra day in camp rather than on the trail, (if you have allotted the extra time to do so). The footing is quite nice with some rock here and there and some roots in areas. Overall, these trails have great footing with sandy dirt mix. Be sure to sign in at any Wilderness or other informational boxes set up by the Forest Service so they know where and who you are and your plans for the ride.

Directions to Whitefish Horse Camp: Drive south on Highway 97 from the town of La Pine. Go about 20 miles more to reach the town of Crescent and the Crescent Cutoff Road (Road 61) go west. Drive on Road 61 for 12.2 miles, then go another 3.5 miles on Highway 58, and finally 6.7 miles more on Road 60. Camp is on the right-hand side of the road across from Crescent Lake.

Whitefish Horse Camp includes: Camp is at 4870'. There are 17 sites, vault toilets, water, tables, fire pits, and manure removal required (bags are provided), nice 4-set corrals at the sites. Operated by Recreation Resource Management Inc. (ReserveUSA.com) call 877.444.6777). There is a fee to stay here (sometimes no fee after Labor Day). Trails from camp include Whitefish Creek #42 and Metolius Windigo #99. Use these to make many loops or trailer a short way to increase your circumference. The Diamond

Peak Wilderness is to the north, northwest and northeast of Whitefish Horse Camp.

For More information contact:

Crescent Ranger District
P.O. Box 208
Crescent, OR 07733
541.433.3200

Maps to use: Diamond Peak Wilderness and USGS Willamette Pass Quadrangle 7.5-minute series (topographic)

Day-off: Josie rides her mountain bike.

Crater Butte #44

(From Snell Lake Trail #43 to Fawn Lake Trail #44A)

Distance: 6.2 Miles	
Altitude: 5632'-6228'	
Maps: Diamond Peak Wilderness and USGS Willamette Pass Topo	
Difficulty: Moderate	

Directions: Use connecting trails, no trailhead to this trail section

Connecting Trails: 42, 44B, 44A, and 48

Horse Camping: Use Whitefish Horse Camp

Trail Description: I rode here in late September when the daylight is shorter than in the summer and was able to cover 6.2 of the 13.7 total miles of Crater Butte Trail #44. You can incorporate this trail to make a nice loop from camp. I will describe it going two opposite directions from Whitefish Creek Trail #42, which is the most popular trail from Whitefish Horse Camp. Ride on Whitefish Creek Trail #42 for 3.7 miles north into the Diamond Peak Wilderness from the far end of camp to the first 4-way intersection. This is where Crater Butte Trail #44 crosses Whitefish Creek Trail #42. First we'll go westward for 1.5 miles to the intersection of Snell Trail #43. Then we will go east for 4.7 miles to Fawn Lake and Fawn Lake Trail #44A. *Going west;* a destination sign reads; "Pacific Crest Trail" with an arrow, ride that direction. You are on Crater Butte Trail #44. Right away you'll ford Whitefish Creek and travel uphill, gently following a drainage passing a seasonal lake. In this valley there are crossings of creeks that may have water in them depending on the time of year you visit. The trail follows the creek drainage. There are some quick views of Diamond Peaks through the trees. It is a combination of wetlands and deep forest by the time you reach Snell Lake Trail #43 turn-off, which is a stark contrast from where we started at the Whitefish Creek Trail #42 intersection where it was high desert land. This trail continues on up to the PCT #2000 (although this trip we turned south here towards Road 6010 on Snell Lake Trail #43). *Going east;* towards Fawn Lake on the Crater Butte Trail #44, you'll find gentle uphill terrain with a view of Diamond Peaks over your left shoulder. There are wooden water bars laid over the trail to help with erosion problems. Ride downhill to a flat open spot where you'll see a hillside to the left and Saddle Lake on the right. It is a beautiful lake with a great sandy beach. Find a log to sit on and enjoy the view as you eat your lunch. Remember to always tie your horses at least 200' from any water source. Mount up, and from here you'll go down about half a dozen switchbacks spaced nicely and enter into deep forest to intersect with Stag Lake Trail #44B (I highly suggest you take time to go see Stag Lake). Continue (after visiting the lake) still on Crater Butte Trail #44 which travels upon a small spine of land with good tread. Travel this ridge area as it heads downhill, flattening out at huge Fawn Lake (shaped like an arrowhead). This is where you'll meet several trails-the first choice being to continue on Crater Butte Trail #44, (we didn't ride the last 3.8 miles to Odell Lake). Another option is to take Fawn Lake Trail #44A going to the left. You'll see the newly signed Pretty Lake Trail #48 to the right going around Fawn Lake (both of these trails can be used to make loops.) This is a great wooded path with lots to see and nice varied terrain to trail ride.

Josie & Ali at Diamond View Lake.

Fawn Lake #44A

Distance: 4.7 Miles	
Altitude: 4800'-5632'	
Maps: Diamond Peak Wilderness and USGS Willamette Pass Topo.	
Difficulty: Moderate	

Directions: Fawn Lake Trailhead is at the north end of Crescent Lake off of paved Road 60. Use the same directions for coming to camp, except turn to the left (south) where the sign reads: Fawn Lake Trailhead / Crescent Lake Camp (people only camp). Turn again at the signed trailhead parking, where you'll find a large circle drive and a nice vault toilet. No camping allowed here. The trail leaves by the toilet area-it is signed.

Connecting Trails: 48 and 44

Horse Camping: Use Whitefish Horse Camp

Trail Description: Begin your trek on Fawn Lake Trail #44A to go see the beautiful Fawn Lake. From the trailhead, go on soft sandy footing in forest and cross paved Road 60. Take a couple steps to cross Metolius Windigo Trail #99. Fawn Lake Trail #44A travels on rolling terrain. At first it is almost all in timberland. At about the 1 mile-point is Pretty Lake Trail #48. It is newly signed by the Forest Service and goes west (left). Next you'll cross what looked like an old road, or perhaps it is a snow slide area. The trail varies from sparse forest to deeper woods. Riding on, Fawn Lake Trail #44A has a steady upward grade to the lake. There is one massive tree that must be 6' in diameter which had fallen across the trail and a new route has been made to go around it. It's awesome to think of the noise it made when it fell, or do you think a tree makes no sound when it falls if no one is around to hear it? The trail bends and contours with the draws on the hillside, going northwest on good tread. A section on the north slope has the tops of the trees sheered off, (and what is left of them resembles toothpicks) and thick dead-fall on the floor. The path changes to a somewhat arid landscape, then returns to lush forest again as you reach the nice size Fawn Lake. The older section of Pretty Lake Trail #48 leaves to the left of Fawn Lake and Crater Butte Trail #44 goes to the right.

*Note: Pretty Lake Trail #48 is shown on the Diamond Peak Wilderness Map as going only from Fawn Lake to Pretty Lake, but it connects to Fawn Lake Trail #44A now on both ends

Meek Lake #43.1

Distance: 2.2 Miles	
Altitude: 5600'-6000'	
Maps: Diamond Peak Wilderness and USGS Willamette Pass Topo.	
Difficulty: Moderate	

Directions: To reach this trail you have two choices. The first is to ride from camp using the Metolius Windigo Trail #99 to Road 6010, then going up the road for about 3.5 miles to the trailhead. The second option is to ride this trail in a loop using the road only to cross from one trail to the next. This trail has a shared trailhead with Snell Lake Trail #43. The Forest Service wants you to know that Road 6010 is not maintained, do not drive on it.

*Note: There is conflicting information whether Meek Lake Trail #43.1 is considered part of Snell Lake Trail #43; however it is signed as Meek Lake Trail at the trailhead.

Connecting Trails: 43, Road 6010, and 46

Horse Camping: Use Whitefish Horse Camp

Trail Description: Starting the ride on Meek Lake Trail #43.1 from Road 6010 you'll go south through somewhat arid terrain and sparse trees. The trail rolls along with good footing. You'll reach Meek Lake soon after you start. It is very nice. We saw so many lakes on our trip, by the time we got to this one it was just another lake, although I know each lake has special aspects. There are several switchbacks here and there. There is an open arid region that looks misplaced. The path takes you to a more lush area in deeper timberland towards the top. The last set of switchbacks travel uphill quickly and are short in length. They are rugged with a few rocks, roots and are somewhat steep. The trail ends at the top at a "T" intersection with Summit Lake Trail #46. Lots of loop options. The mid section of the trail and the upper end towards Summit Lake Trail #46 look as if Mouther Nature must have exploded. There were trees, and debris knocked in every direction all over the gullies and depressions in the ground. The trail wound around all of this chaos. There were seasonal ponds that were dry in late

September when we visited. This is the most unusual trail in the area.

*Note: The Diamond Peak Wilderness Map reads that there is a footbridge going over Summit Creek in Meek Lake Trail, but the bridge is actually on Summit Lake Trail.

Josie and Ali at Darleen Lake.

Metolius Windigo #99

Distance: 4.6 Miles ridden this trip (17.3 Miles total in this area)

Altitude: 4870'-4900'

Maps: Diamond Peak Wilderness and USGS Willamette Pass Topo.

Difficulty: Moderate

Directions: Metolius Windigo Trailhead is located at the far end of camp where the camp road makes a loop. There is a small day-park area. From the trailhead on Metolius Windigo Trail #99 you can go either northeast towards Fawn Lake Trail #44A or go south towards Road 6010 and Windy Lakes Trail #50. This is also Whitefish Creek Trailhead, which goes northward. You may also catch the Metolius Windigo Trail #99 from near the entrance of camp, both areas are signed.

Connecting Trails: 42, 44A, Road 6010, and 50

Horse Camping: Use Whitefish Horse Camp

Trail Description: Metolius Windigo Trail #99 goes along the edge of Whitefish Horse Camp. It will be described in two directions. *Going towards Fawn Lake Trail #44A;* take Metolius Windigo Trail #99 from camp at the end of the loop at the shared trailhead with Whitefish Creek Trail #42 and head right. It rolls along a hillside for 3.6 miles paralleling Crescent Lake and Road 60 below. The trail stays in deep timberland and is nice and shady. It goes downhill slightly to cross Fawn Lake Trail #44A where most people turn to make a loop or continue on to reach Crescent Lake Sno Park. *Going towards Windy Lakes Trail #50;* take Metolius Windigo Trail #99 from camp from the above shared trailhead with Whitefish Creek Trail #42 and go to the left behind the campsites. If you are parked in the lower section of camp use the trailhead at the entrance to camp instead. This section is short, about 1 mile or so, and helps to connect Road 6010, Windy Lakes #50 and Oldenberg Lake #45 Trails for loops. Start from camp under a canopy of dense woods traveling over a bridge and up onto a bluff overlooking Road 60 and Crescent Lake. The path goes along Road 6010 a short way, then crosses it, goes through the woods and connects to Windy Lakes Trail #50.

Oldenberg Lake #45

(To Summit Lake Trail #46)

Distance: 5 Miles
Altitude: 5000'-5500'
Maps: Diamond Peak Wilderness and USGS Willamette Pass Topo.
Difficulty: Moderate

Directions: You can either ride Metolius Windigo Trail #99 south out of camp towards Windy Lakes Trail #50 to jump on Oldenberg Lake Trail #45 or drive to the trailhead off Road 60. Go past the horse camp on paved Road 60. As it goes uphill take a left onto a small road to a signed trailhead at the southwest end of Crescent Lake. There is a circular road and a big trailhead with a vault toilet. There is another trailhead further down Road 60, but we did not drive to it, although we saw the unmarked spur trail going down to it when we rode Oldenberg Lake Trail #45.

Connecting Trails: 50, unmarked spur, and 46

Horse Camping: Use Whitefish Horse Camp

Trail Description: Oldenberg Lake Trail #45 is actually 9.7 miles, but we incorporated about 5 miles of it in our loop from camp. Using this trail to connect Windy Lakes Trail #50 to Summit Lake Trail #46 you'll see an increase in elevation towards the south at Oldenberg Lake and the end of Summit Lake Trail #46. There are arid forests, seasonal creeks (one had a bridge) , and a couple of lakes (one of course being Oldenberg Lake) as well as Bingham Lakes and a pond or two with marshy sides. Some are okay to water at and have trails down to the shoreline. There are views-look between the trees to see Diamond Peak and Crescent Lake. Near Crescent Lake there is an unmarked trail, which goes down to a road and another trailhead. Overall this is a nice stroll but it is one of the least interesting trails. However, you can make good time on it and it helps to make a loop!

HORSES ON THE LOOSE

One summer day I got a call from a riding buddy. She said she had received an odd request for help from some gals that had gone camping up at Haney Meadow / Ken Wilcox Horse Camp. My friend relayed the story the gals had told her of how they had gone for a ride late in the day and had stopped for a break. One horse got loose, then the other, and they ran away through the forest. They wanted help in finding them as quick as possible. The girls were tired because they were up all night the previous night looking for the horses. We loaded up our horses and headed out. We arrived kind of late in the day ourselves. It was about 3-4 o'clock in the afternoon. The girls were not in camp. A man told us they had gotten a hold of him and he had brought them some horses and that the girls had taken off on the search. We went as fast as we could. (I know the area very well.) My riding buddy was a very willing partner to help to go look for these animals. We found items that had come off of their saddles-food and drinks. However we did not have any luck with the animals. We found only empty hoof-prints. Time was not on our side so we rode about 15 miles and figured that was as good as we could do. The next day my friend posted signs in the bottom of Naneum Canyon. A rancher then saw her sign and drove up to a gated road that had a cattle guard where he thought the horses might be. Tah-dah, he was right! Later my riding buddy got a call from the girls. They were on their way home after getting the horses from the bottom of the canyon, which was all of the way down on the north side of Ellensburg, Washington! The saddles stayed on and the horses were unharmed. The rancher said if horses get loose and have a choice, they will always go downhill. I guess he was right.

Pretty Lake #48

Distance: 3.5	
Altitude: 5632'-5811'	
Maps: Diamond Peak Wilderness and USGS Willamette Pass Topo.	
Difficulty: Moderate	

Directions: Begins and ends off Fawn Lake Trail

Connecting Trail: 44A

Horse Camping: Use Whitefish Horse Camp

Trail Description: Pretty Lake Trail #48 is attached at both ends to Fawn Lake Trail #44A, so you can begin either at the north end at Fawn Lake or from the southeast end off of Fawn Lake Trail #44A. The trail goes steadily uphill from either end, however more-so from the southeast end. (There used to only be a trail from Fawn Lake to Pretty Lake, but now the trail connects down the other side of the ridge to Fawn Lake Trail #44A as well.) I'll describe the trek from Fawn Lake. Starting at the lake, Pretty Lake Trail #48 goes along the southeast and then the south side of Fawn Lake on great footing in deep timber. You can see nice views of three peaks-Lakeview Mountain at 7066', an unnamed one in the center standing at 6892', and on the far left sits Redtop Mountain at 6948'. Ride up a switchback, then down to an arid spot and up once more. Glance at a small green lake sitting below on the left. This gleaming beauty is Pretty Lake and you are now at the 1.5 mile-point. This is where the trail ends according to some maps. (The topographical map does show it continuing.) The remainder of the trail descends to where you'll notice the nice new water bars (wooden short poles set in the ground cross-wise to help with erosion) across the path. It is about 1.5 miles from the top down to reach Fawn Lake Trail #44A. It is steady downhill, but not too steep, with good tread, all in timberland. The "T" intersection at the bottom with Fawn Lake Trail #44A was not signed when we visited, but the Forest Service has put in new signs. Road 60 is only about ½ mile or so to the right on Fawn Lake Trail #44A.

Road 6010

Distance: 4.5 Miles (To Summit Lake)
Altitude: 5000'-5600'
Maps: Diamond Peak Wilderness and USGS Willamette Pass Topo.
Difficulty: Moderate

Directions: Take Metolius Windigo Trail #99 from camp to the south for about .5 mile to where it crosses Road 6010. Turn right on this road. This is a gated road and is not maintained.

Connecting Trails: 99, 43.1, 43, and 46

Horse Camping: Use Whitefish Horse Camp

Trail Description: Road 6010 is used to connect the 4 trails listed above, so I thought that it would be helpful to include a description of it. It is a nice road to ride on with fabulous footing, (soft and sandy) which makes a great warm up or cool down as it is not too steep. It heads uphill from where Metolius Windigo Trail #99 crosses it by Crescent Lake to the shared trailhead of Snell Lake #43 and Meek Lake #43.1. This is the high point of the road. This road is not maintained and not suitable for rigs. It rolls downhill towards Summit Lake and Summit Lake Trail #46 and its trailhead. We enjoyed riding the road and thought it was an excellent way to get to and from the surrounding trails from camp.

John, Robin, and Donna J. enjoy the mountain lake.

Diamond Peaks

Snell Lake #43

Distance: 5.3 Miles

Altitude: 5600'-6050'

Maps: Diamond Peak Wilderness and USGS Willamette Pass Topo.

Difficulty: Moderate

Directions: Ride on Road 6010 from Road 60 for about 3 miles to the shared trailhead of Snell Lake #43 and Meek Lake #43.1 (Road 6010 is gated and not maintained for rigs).

Connecting Trails: 43.1, 44, and Road 6010

Horse Camping: Use Whitefish Horse Camp

Trail Description: From Road 6010, sign in at the Diamond Peak Wilderness station and head out on the beautiful woodland Snell Lake Trail #43. It travels just over 5 miles going north to the "T" intersection with Crater Butte Trail #44. Start by going gently downhill to the first lake, ride above and around wetlands and over a small bridge that straddles some mud. Rolling trail takes you across a seasonal wash which was missing a culvert when we visited, but was dry as a bone in late September. Ride upward on a switchback to more open terrain on a hillside. You'll enjoy lakes on both sides of the trail, one of which is Effy Lake, then cross a muddy spot. Ride up and around knolls and meet with another lake. It was late in the riding season and the sun felt wonderful along this trail as it lay on our backs. Long switchbacks take you up to views to south of all the surrounding peaks, with yet another blue gem of a lake alongside the trail. You'll ford a seasonal creek twice. Next, the path goes by big rock piles. Three stairs take you down to cross an outlet for a lake. We stopped in a wonderful open grassy spot for lunch. The warm sunny glen was a welcome sight and we lingered with the fall sun rays for as long as we dared, due to shorter riding hours. We found a hidden water hole for the horses to drink out of. Continue on with another set of stairs cut out of the land. The trail takes you by a rivulet of water from yet another lake! Ride on an open hill with views of Diamond Peaks and then down to meet with Crater Butte Trail #44 where you can continue to the right to make a loop back towards camp or to the left headed toward the Pacific Crest National Scenic Trail #2000. Overall we found the Snell Lake Trail #43 to be a fantastic trail with deep-rooted evergreens and pristine lakes. It makes you feel miniature with the large rocks and enormous trees towering above and the footing is like all the other trails around this area, <u>wonderful</u>!

Stag Lake #44B

Distance: .7 Mile
Altitude: 5834'-5920'
Maps: Diamond Peak Wilderness and USGS Willamette Pass Topo.
Difficulty: Moderate

Directions: Access from below connecting trail.

Connecting Trail: 44

Horse Camping: Use Whitefish Horse Camp

Trail Description: Stag Lake is located between Whitefish Creek Trail #42 and Fawn Lake Trail #44A it chutes off of Crater Butte Trail #44. Go north on Stag Lake Trail #44B from Crater Butte Trail #44. Ride downhill, and then up slightly to flatten and roll more, coming to a big pond or small lake-however you see it. You'll reach the bigger Stag Lake with an awesome view of Lakeview Mountain standing at 7066' in the backdrop. The trail ends at the lake and my friend and I agreed this is "A must see" view.

Josie on Ali with trail dog Buddy at Stag Lake.

Summit Lake #46

Distance: 10.9 Miles

Altitude: 6200'-5450'

Maps: Diamond Peak Wilderness and USGS Willamette Pass Topo.

Difficulty: Moderate

Directions: You'll need to ride Road 6010 from paved Road 60 near camp 5 miles to Summit Lake and Summit Lake Trailhead #46. The Forest Service says, "We don't maintain Road 6010 because it's part of a historical military road". You can incorporate this trail in a loop either in one big ride, or since it has many connecting trails, break it into sections and make it a multi-day event. The trailhead at Summit Lake has ample parking and an outhouse with a nice view across Summit Lake with several peaks in the background.

Connecting Trails: Road 6010, 43.1, 50, and 45

Horse Camping: Use Whitefish Horse Camp

Trail Description: I am describing Summit Lake Trail #46 from Road 6010 at Summit Lake and the Summit Lake Trailhead going southeast to the end of the trail at Oldenberg Lake Trail #45. My friend and I found roots and soft footing along the trail near Summit Lake. The bushes and trees were glistening with yesterday's rain drops, so we were glad we wore our rain-gear as often times you get drenched from the water soaked foliage. More so than as if it was an actual rainfall. The logs were steaming as the early morning's sun rays warmed and illuminated the downfall. It looked like a page from a story book-it felt heavenly and smelled earthy. Ride along this peaceful path passing tiny ponds with lily pads floating in the pools. Ride gently down and around the east shoreline of Summit Lake, over the bridge to see wetlands and then travel on rolling terrain though the forest. There are lots of lakes with one having a newly fixed culvert to cross on the outlet. Good job Forest Service and youth crew! There are switchbacks here and there. Intersect with Meek Lake Trail #43.1 which leaves to the left. The miles go quickly and in 2 miles more you'll be at Windy Lakes. Go by a pond and ascend by a rock pile over a small ridge with more lakes including North and East Windy Lakes (signed).

You'll come to another intersection. This time it goes to the right and is a 1 mile trail to South Windy Lakes. It is a short ride to meet the next connecting trail which is Windy Lakes Trail #50 coming in from the left (northeast). From here, still on Summit Lake Trail #46, you'll continue toward Oldenberg Lake Trail #45. Rolling terrain takes you on a delightful trek through the woods passing the beautiful Suzanne and Darlene Lakes. The latter is where we were able to get our horses a drink, with a nice view across the lake of a peak. Both of these lakes are signed. There is a nice lunch spot along side the trail. Look for a snag with a sign on it reading "View of Diamond Peak". The view is a bit limited due to trees but it is visible. The landscape becomes more arid the further you go. Work your way down to the end of the trail to a "T" intersection with Oldenberg Lake Trail #45. Oldenberg Lake is straight ahead from the intersection. This is one of my favorite trails for this area even though it is not inside the Diamond Peak Wilderness.

*Note: The Diamond Peak Wilderness Map reads that there is a foot bridge going over Summit Creek on Meek Lake Trail, but it is actually on Summit Lake Trail.

Crescent Lake

Whitefish Creek #42

(From Whitefish Horse Camp to Diamond View Lake)

Distance: 4 Miles
Altitude: 4870'-5820'
Maps: Diamond Peak Wilderness and USGS Willamette Pass Topo.
Difficulty: Moderate

Directions: You'll find the Whitefish Creek Trailhead at the far end of camp in the loop section. It is signed. This is also the trailhead for the Metolius Windigo Trail #99. There is limited day parking and an outhouse. Whitefish Creek Trail #42 goes basically north.

Connecting Trails: 99 and 44

Horse Camping: Use Whitefish Horse Camp

Trail Description: I'm describing a 4 mile section from Whitefish Horse Camp to Diamond View Lake on the Whitefish Creek Trail #42. (The total length of this trail extends 14.3 miles to Odell Lake. I just didn't have time to do all of it on this trip.) Leave camp on a very gentle uphill grade with a couple of switchbacks up over a knoll with the seasonal Whitefish Creek on your left. Cross a dirt-covered culvert over a small creek where you can easily get your mount a drink. Ride rolling terrain to meet with Crater Butte Trail #44. Cross over it, and continue still on Whitefish Creek Trail #42. Go a short way to see the first lake in the area which has a nice view to the east of Lakeview Mountain 7006'. Cross a log bridge and go see the next lake, Diamond View Lake. It has the best view of Diamond Peak in the whole area! The peak is on the far side of the lake to the west. I think the sunlight of morning would make the best pictures. From camp the trees are sparse and the ground is dry and sandy and the closer you get to the the lakes the greener and lusher it becomes with some moisture in the ground. Bring your camera, go on a clear day and enjoy this trip.

Windy Lakes #50

Distance: 6.7 Miles	
Altitude: 5000'-6000'	
Maps: Diamond Peak Wilderness and USGS Willamette Pass Topo.	
Difficulty: Moderate	

Directions: Go past the horse camp on paved Road 60. As it goes uphill you'll take a left onto a small road to a signed trailhead. This is at the southwest end of Crescent Lake. There is a circular road and a big trailhead with a vault toilet. We found it easier to ride from camp on the Metolius Windigo Trail #99 going south (use the trailhead at the entrance to camp) and you'll head right to the sign guiding you to Windy Lakes Trail #50.

Connecting Trails: 99, 45, and 46

Horse Camping: Use Whitefish Horse Camp

Trail Description: Either way you start this ride, after the intersection with the Metolius Windigo Trail #99, the Windy Lakes Trail #50 heads gently uphill with rubber and wooden water bars across the trail (helps keep erosion to a minimum). It follows the seasonal creek drainage. A half-dozen switchbacks are well placed and help you ascend to a flatter area in deep woods where the path goes up again using a switchback. Ride along a hillside and go up a draw/canyon with a grey rock wall and boulders. Cross a small bridge and climb with the aid of one switchback. This trail makes you feel small. We visited when there was a dusting of snow and the trail was covered in places with ice which made it both interesting and beautiful, as well as a little nerve racking. Summit Lake Trail #46 "T" intersects at the end of the line. Go either way to complete a loop in the area. This is an interesting trail. South Windy Lake is a nice little 1 mile trail that can be added onto your excursion by riding south off Summit Lake Trail #46. Go uphill around and down contouring a bigger one of the Windy Lakes. This is a lesser traveled path. Ride on, passing one, and then another lake. South Windy Lake has a good watering spot for the horses and a pleasant sandy shoreline. It was a good side trail to take on a beautiful fall ride.

FREMONT NATIONAL FOREST
(Silver Creek Marsh, Antler Trailhead, and Farm Well Horse Camps)

Fremont National Forest is located in south central Oregon in the Outback Region. The terrain is wide-ranging. Sometimes you'll find yourself in high mountain timberland riding toward a lookout and other times you'll be in flatter high desert areas with prehistoric craters or dry lake beds with dust devils swirling about your head. There are lakes of all dimensions, with cold streams and abrasive volcanic areas to tantalize your senses. You can visit a rural hot spring or grab a bite at an out-of-the way diner in a one-gas station town. I highly recommend a visit to The Cowboy Dinner Tree Steakhouse which has no electricity and is very rustic; decorated with old tack, saddles, and ancient relics. Visit the weathered out-building made into their gift shop and buy a keepsake to take home, or take a turn at roping the straw steer with the plastic head. Reservations are needed, so call them for times and days. They offer a choice of beef or chicken. (I ordered chicken and they served me a whole one!) You also get a huge drink of

pink lemonade and big rolls, homemade bean soup, salad, baked potato and for dessert, raspberry shortcake all for a measly $23.50. Some people ride from camp and tie up to a rail, but our reservations were at 7:00 P.M. and my friend and I didn't want to ride next to the paved road in the dark. Bring cash. They also have cabins for rent. Whatever your pleasure, you are sure to find something to delight you in the Oregon Outback Region. The riding is diverse so if you are looking for a thrilling hard ride or a soft pleasure ride you'll find it here. We were able to ride 9 hour days, putting long slow miles on my green-broke horse by using a combination of trails and roads. Put on your walking-pants and happy-feet and enjoy your vacation. Do your homework and always call ahead for trail conditions as they change from year to year due to weather, fire, runoff, and usage. The horse camps are nice and have corrals. Silver Creek Marsh is a lower elevation camp at 4800' and Antler Trailhead Horse Camp is higher at 6400'. There is a trail that connects these two camps. There is another camp called Farm Well Horse Camp which is to the east of Silver Creek Marsh Horse Camp. That has an elevation of 5100', and has a more challenging section of the National Recreation Trail system with a 4-5 mile long trail which goes to Hager Mountain Lookout. The Silver Lake Ranger District was so kind as to mail me a map showing the trail clearing that had been completed as of the date we were to arrive. The National Recreation Trail #160 is broken into sections- Auger, (Hager Mountain), Yamsay and Silver Creek. In the future, the Forest Service says the segments are going to be changed from assigned numbers (as they currently are) to naming them as one whole trail.

Directions to Silver Creek Marsh Horse Camp: Silver Creek Marsh Horse Camp is located near the town of Silver Lake. I'll describe how to get here coming from the west. Take Highway 97 to Highway 31, (which is south of LaPine), and drive toward the town of Silver Lake. Just before reaching the town, you will see a bend in the road that you can use as a landmark to turn onto paved

Josie and her horse Breezy and trail dog Daisy take a rest in the hot afternoon.

County Road 4-11. This road turns into Forest Service Road 27. Go about 11 miles to Silver Creek Marsh Horse Camp. Camp is on the left side of the road.

Silver Creek Marsh Horse Camp includes: Camp was free when I visited, although there is a proposed fee starting in 2009 of $6.00 per night. For stock water, use West Fork Silver Creek that flows to the east of camp. There is a hand pump for water (the handle was broken off, but the Forest Service said it will be repaired by the summer of 2009). You'll find big, tall corrals; one 4-horse and one 2-horse. The other sites have hitchin' rails and there is a spot by the corrals for placing your horse's droppings. There are 8 sites designed for horses, and 5 with no designation. Several are drive-through spots and there is lots of room for extra vehicles or over-sized rigs. To the east of camp are Silver Creek Marsh and a meadow. Also available are cute vault toilets with little porches and inside each one there is wood paneling that smelled fresh and clean. There is a day-use area with big and small BBQ stands with griddles. You'll find tables and fire pits with grates too. There are old trails to make note of-one goes across the marsh/ meadow and the other is near the entrance to camp across the paved road. Both are not in use now. For more details on reroutes, read each trail listed in this chapter. This is a spacious camp set under tall Ponderosa trees. The area around camp was severely burned in 2002. The trails go in and out of

Another blow-out!!

the places that were in the path of destruction, but camp was spared. Be cautious of loose soil around stumps and burnt trees. You can create a nasty hole by stepping on top of an invisible tunnel made from incinerated roots. The trees that are burned can come toppling down without notice, even when the wind is not blowing. There were several significant crashes when my friend and I visited. There are two trails leaving from camp that branch off in different directions. One trail goes southwest up a draw following the West Fork Silver Creek to Antler Trailhead Horse Camp and then to

Yamsay Mountain. The other trail goes east to Hager Mountain Lookout, and down the other side of the mountain to end at Farm Well Horse Camp.

Directions to Antler Trailhead Horse Camp: Antler Trailhead Horse Camp is located near the town named Silver Lake. I'll describe the directions coming from the west. Take Highway 97 to Highway 31 (which is south of LaPine), and drive toward the town of Silver Lake. Starting just west of the town of Silver Lake on Highway 31 you will turn south on County Road 4-11 which turns into Forest Service Road 27. Take Forest Service Road 27 for 9 miles, and then turn right onto Forest Service Road 2804. Go 2.5 miles to Forest Service Road 7645, turn left and drive 5 miles to Forest Service Road 036. Turn left on Forest Service Road 036 and go 2.3 miles. Turn right onto Forest Service Road 038 and drive .6 mile up to the trailhead. There is a loop in camp or park in the day parking area near the toilet.

Antler Horse Camp includes: There are 4 corrals at one camp, 5 hitchin' rails, a nice water pump, 1 vault toilet, a manure heap, fire rings with grates, tables, a day use area, and 5 sites that are pull-in which are nice and level. Camp elevation is at 6400'.

Directions to Farm Well Horse Camp: Farm Well Horse Camp is located near the town named Silver Lake. I'll describe the directions coming from the west. Take Highway 97 to Highway 31 (which is south of LaPine) and drive toward the town of Silver Lake. Leaving from the Town of Silver Lake, drive about 6 miles on paved County Road 4-12 which turns into Forest Service Road 28 (you will pass by the Cowboy Dinner Tree Restaurant). Turn left onto Forest Service Road 2916 and go about 6 miles more. Camp is on the left-hand side of the road.

Farm Well Horse Camp includes: There are 6 camp sites with 14 corrals. One of the sites is a pull-through type. The camp offers picnic tables, grills, vault toilet, and stock pond for water. Check ahead for the availability of potable water, the Forest Service said it is proposed for 2010. The setting is quite pleasant as it is a long ways from any major road and is quiet. I did not stay here this trip. We scouted out this camp on our way to dinner at "The Cowboy Dinner Tree Steakhouse". We came from Silver Creek Marsh Horse Camp. You may access a couple of trails from Farm Well Horse Camp. One is National Recreation Trail #17 (NRT #160), and the other one is Hager Mountain #18 (NRT #160) which goes to the top of

Josie and her mare along Silver Creek.

Bridge over Silver Creek.

A big rock outcropping on Scenic Rock Loop Trail.

Hager Mountain and then connects down to Silver Creek Marsh Horse Camp. Farm Well Horse Camp is at 5100'. You should call ahead to check the conditions of the trails. They were re-routed because of the 2002 fire, and the Forest Service said it was cleared in 2008.

For More information contact:

Silver Lake Ranger District
P.O. Box 129
Silver Lake, OR 97638
541-576-2107

Maps to use: Fremont National Forest and Oregon Road & Recreation Atlas

Contact information for The Cowboy Dinner Tree Steakhouse:
Don & Connie Ramage
P.O. Box 44
Silver Lake, Oregon 97638
541-576-2426
www.cowboydinnertree.net

Barb and George on their mules.

Trail dog, Daisy.

Hager Mountain #18 (NRT #160)

Distance: 14 Miles	
Altitude: 4800'-7183'	
Maps: Oregon Road & Recreation Atlas and Fremont National Forest	
Difficulty: Moderate-Challenging (steep near top & down to Farm Well Camp)	

Directions: You can start this trail from either Silver Creek Marsh Horse Camp or from Farm Well Horse Camp as well as a spot along Road 28 where there is a small spot to park.

Horse Camping: Silver Creek Horse Camp or Farm Well Horse Camp.

Trail Description: We only rode our horses on a 4 mile section of this trail going from Silver Creek Marsh Horse Camp to Road 28. This section of the NRT #160 I'll call "Auger". The plan was to complete this trail to the lookout. However, I was on a green broke horse and decided not to push the envelope. We heard the top section of the trail is pretty challenging. Hager Mountain Trail #18 (NRT #160) will be described starting from Silver Creek Marsh Camp. Use the newer trailhead across from the 4-corral camp site through the green gate. Follow the trail alongside the road to the south where it dumps you out on the paved road. Go around the culvert and creek, then back down to the trail again. Stay on the same side of the pavement (do not cross the paved road). Portions of this trail are old 2-track and parts are single tread. There is a sign to guide you which reads "NRT #160 Hager Mt. Tr. #18". Follow an old 2-track at this point which then becomes a single trail. Be watchful for emblems marking the trail with USA inside of a triangle and look for rock cairns as well. We found ribbons too. The trail is well forested. You'll notice a logged-off area and then you'll go through 2 small gates. Pass along fence lines down to a pole-line area and follow open grassy meadows with a small rocky spot. This is where you'll meet up with another 2-track to head east (right). There is no sign here so remember this turn if you are coming back this way. We missed it and made the ride a lot longer. Follow the road around a few curves and then look for the trail marker on the right as the path goes up an embankment (if you miss this turn you'll end up near a red cinder road and a swampy area). The trail goes up, then rolls along an open area through a green gate and then rolls some more. This trail, overall, has good footing. You'll find yourself at the top of a steep canyon with Silver Creek running in the bottom. Silver Creek is the drainage from Thompson Reservoir. Switchback down a couple times, then go along a hillside, gently following the slope. At the bottom there is a cool bridge with sides on it. It is quite long. Looking underneath you can see it is supported by a huge boulder. Here the trail follows alongside the stream for about a ½ mile or so then you'll see a sign marking a path to Auger Camp. We had lunch at the little camp, which is beautiful. The stream is wide and has a huge meadow on the other side. There is a fire ring, a table and a small road. We found it to be a wonderful spot to water our mounts and lounge around. This would be a nice destination if you like to pack-in. You can drive into this site from Road 28. The far side of the stream has views of open hills dotted with charred trees from an old burn. After lunch we headed back out and went up the other side of the canyon on less steep terrain. There are several switchbacks that are well-placed to help you reach the top of the gorge. The rest of this 4-mile section of trail is nondescript, with open terrain and some trees. It crosses paved Forest Service Road 28. There is a pull-off by the trail big enough for 1 or 2 rigs. Someone told us that the small road by Auger camp can be ridden all the way to the reservoir.

*Note: This trail is part of the National Recreation Trail #160 I have broken it into sections Auger- (Hager Mountain), Yamsay and Silver Creek . In the future the Forest Service says the segments are going to be changed from assigned (as they currently are) to naming them as one whole trail.

Leave gates how you find them.

Scenic Rock Loop

Distance: 2 Miles
Altitude: 6400'-6600'
Maps: Oregon Road & Recreation Atlas and Fremont National Forest
Difficulty: Moderate

Directions: Follow the directions at the beginning of the chapter for Antler Trailhead Horse Camp.

Connecting Trails: Yamsay Mountain Lookout #18 (NRT #160) and Silver Creek (NRT #160)

Horse Camping: Antler Trailhead Horse Camp.

Trail Description: You'll find the signed trailhead for Scenic Rock Loop Trail located near the toilet at Antler Trailhead Horse Camp. The other end of this loop trail is located behind the corrals which is a shared trailhead with Silver Creek Trail. We will start at the trailhead by the toilet area. I liked riding through forest, all the time on a bright new trail. It smelled so fresh up at this altitude. The NYC crew had been working on the trail a few days before we arrived in camp, so we felt privileged to go on the newly cleared path. It goes uphill with nice footing to reach an awesome stand of rocks jutting out of the ground with tired, old, dead trees leaning on them. Follow the trail downhill to a sign-"Red Shasta Fir" which is an ancient enormous tree. Ride downhill some more to an intersection. This is Yamsay Mountain Lookout Trail (NRT #160) which leaves to the right. (It was unmarked with the sign just reading "Antler Trailhead", with an arrow.) Now you'll begin looping back toward camp through nice green meadows. There is another intersection with a sign and mileage. This time it reads "Silver Creek Trail 6, Antler Spring and Yamsay Mountain 8 ½ ". Next is a sign for the NYC Green Crew 2008 to signify their efforts put fourth for cleaning this fine trail. Continue on Scenic Rook Loop Trail which ends back in Antler Trailhead Horse Camp where there is a post-marker listed as "Easiest" designating this trail. The trail ends near the corrals. It is a shared trailhead for both Silver Creek Trail (NRT #160) and Scenic Rock Loop Trail. There is another trail out of camp marked "Hiker" that is just a tie trail to Silver Creek Trail (NRT #160).

Silver Creek (NRT #160)

Distance: 6 Miles
Altitude: 4800'-6400'
Maps: Oregon Road & Recreation Atlas and Fremont National Forest
Difficulty: Moderate

Directions: This trail begins from Silver Creek Marsh Horse Camp. On the west side of camp, directly across the paved road, go through the green gate. You'll find a sign reading Antler Trailhead. This is the Silver Creek Trail.

Connecting Trails: Scenic Rock Loop and Yamsay Mountain Lookout #18 (NRT #160)

Horse Camping: Silver Creek Marsh or Antler Trailhead Horse Camps

Trail Description: Silver Creek Trail goes between Silver Creek Marsh Horse Camp and Antler Trailhead Horse Camp. It is part of NRT #160. I rode it starting from Silver Creek Marsh Horse Camp. Begin by riding west, cross the paved camp road and go through the green gate. Here there is a destination sign reading; "Yamsay Mt. 14 miles and Antler TH 6 miles". Follow the trail. The next part was not marked very well. Just ride along-side the main paved road, and then go west across Forest Service Road 27 to dirt Road 292 which also has a gate. Be sure to close the gate after entering. Go approximately ¼ mile on the little dirt road. Veer onto a single track trail (marked by a rock cairn) which leaves to the south. The trail marker emblem is a triangle shape with big USA letters in the center and National Recreational Trail written on the bottom. It is, of course, colored red, white and blue for the good old USA. Follow the trail from the road and go left (south). Ride up an open brushy hill and back down to the North Fork Silver Creek drainage where there is lush foliage. The brook is beautiful and makes a nice babbling sound. You'll ride on a gradually climbing trail. You will notice a blackened old burn area that strikes a contrast to the brushy green undergrowth. The trail is good, with some rocks and a stream that you will cross twice. The first crossing is a ford with a separate log for foot travelers. The second time you cross this intimate creek is on a side-less bridge built in 2008. The Forest Service says two bridges were built in 2008 at Two Creek. One-"Hiker Only" and one- "Horse Bridge". The trail becomes more serious about ascending with the help of a few switchbacks. The South Fork Silver Creek will be further away once you get up the hillside where the trail levels out more. The clearing crew must have been there recently, because the path was almost swept clean and was well maintained. Ride through another green metal gate and continue onward, still slightly uphill. My friend and I were turned around when we came upon red tape strung across the trail, signaling that travel beyond this point was severely discouraged. We had a Forest Service map that did indicate that the trail was not completely cleared, but we had to give it a go. We rode about 4 miles on this trail. Overall the trail was a great one. If you have old maps, be sure to take note of the newer beginning of this trail. The old trail starts in a slightly different spot closer to the entrance of Silver Creek Marsh Horse Camp. We found that the old sign was still up, but read "Trail closed". It took some looking to find the new route.

*Note: This trail is part of the National Recreation Trail #160 I have broken it into sections Auger- (Hager Mountain), Yamsay and Silver Creek. In the future, the Forest Service says the segments are going to be changed from assigned numbers (as they currently are) to naming them as one whole trail.

Josie and Breezy

Yamsay Mountain Lookout #18 (NRT #160)

Distance: 8.5 Miles

Altitude: 6400'-8100'

Maps: Oregon Road & Recreation Atlas and Fremont National Forest

Difficulty: Moderate

Directions: Follow the directions at the beginning of the chapter for Antler Trailhead Horse Camp.

Connecting Trail: Scenic Rock Loop

Horse Camping: Antler Trailhead Horse Camp.

Trail Description: I was only able to complete 4.5 miles of this trail due to a late start. I was alone so I decided not to push my luck and end up coming back in the dark. I can say that the first 4.5 miles of this 8.5 mile trail is in the "Moderate" level of trail difficultly. To start this trail, go behind the corrals at Antler Trailhead Horse Camp to the shared trailhead of Silver Creek Trail (NRT #160) and Scenic Rock Loop Trail. Take the Scenic Rock Loop Trail, going west for about ½ mile where you'll come upon a sign guiding you toward Yamsay Mountain. At the next intersection, the sign reads "Loop Trail" which goes north. You will turn west (Left) on the unmarked path. This is Yamsay Mountain Lookout Trail #18 (NRT #160). Going uphill, it is a continuous climb through pine forest and has nice sandy soil with lavender colored rocks here and there. Ride up switchbacks placed intermittently, to a pile of big rocks. The trail continues on up, then levels and, then up some more to a look-about spot. Here there is a hand-made bench made out of logs to sit on and ponder the view to the east of Hager Mountain Lookout. Far off you'll see Silver Lake, with Sycan Marsh way beyond. The trail levels for a bit going around a hill then down to a meadow which would be a nice spot to pack-in to. Here there is feed and water in Long Creek for the horses. Ford the creek next to the foot bridge and climb up on a hillside in deep dark woods on a wide trail with nice footing. Ride up and around into a sparsely forested region with sandy footing. It is a very arid area. You can see some small views to the west of far-off Three Sisters Mountains and what I surmised as the Yamsay Mountain Lookout. The trail was descending when I made my decision and although I wanted to continue, I had to return back to camp due to a late start. How about you finishing this trail and tell me about it?! Maybe I can return to this magnificent area some day.

The Forest Service has graciously finished this trail description for us. "From the last point with the overview of the Cascades, the trail continues going west along a high top bench traveling through lodge pole pine stands with very little underbrush;. The soils are pumice and very easy riding through this portion. Continue down towards Antler Springs. You'll intersect with an old road crossing. It was used years ago for folks traveling from the main roads. (Now it has been made into a trail, which goes two ways; to the left to Blue Buck Springs (3 miles) and to the right to Antler Springs nestled in a small, beautiful meadow). The NRT #160 crosses here where the sign shows viewpoint 1 mile and Yamsay Lookout site 3.8 miles. Continue through flat pumice ground with lodge pole stands, winding through to the west, then climbs a bit through Shasta fir and lodge pole stands. Here along a large bluff for ¼ mile you have views of Buck Meadows, 700' below, and the Cascade Mountains in the background. The trail turns down to the left through heavy pumice soils with a lot of rutted drainages that have no ground cover and over story pine (short too). It winds to the right at the bottom of this bench and intersects with a game trail used by wildlife like bears, mountain lions, elk, and deer (connecting Long Creek drainage to the left and Buck Meadows to the right). Here you'll continue west with a gradual climb where basalt rock out-crops show up. You will then come to a spot where meadows appear. This is a great place to camp. Or, make it a base camp, then venture up the east side of the Yamsay Crater. This site is the headwaters of Long Creek and Buck Creek, which comes out of the same water source. Pure water... but still boil it when in doubt. Here the trail goes northwest, gradually climbing up through pumice soil and pine tree stands until you break out to open areas on the east side of Yamsay Crater. The trail uses an existing old Indian trail from here to the top of Yamsay, about 1 mile away. The spot just to the left has a viewpoint. Here you can see into the one meadow below, around 800' down. In this crater you'll notice the huge ancient bulge in the center, just like Mount Saint Helens had when the volcanic mountain built its last bulge. The view continues over the west rim to the Cascades, and from Mount Scott, clear through to the Sisters Mountains...grand view. From here, continue to the south and gradually ascend towards Yamsay Peak. Here is the remaining site of the Forest Service lookout. Historically there are remnants of a ladder lookout just to the east of the old foundation supports and next to the rim. Trees have grown through the ladder, with

Jane & Beau.

C.J. and Dot enjoy their ride.

galvanized wire from the 1920's still attached to it. The Yamsay Lookout top had at least two or three structures for fire detection over the years and many names have been added to the remaining supports. The road that came up to the top has been closed and blocked since the 1980's. The old rock wall near the top is a beautiful example of the work done from the CCC days of the 1930's. The trail no longer continues to go west to meet the Pacific Crest Trail #2000 due to the Klamath Tribe's concern for this mountain, which is sacred to the peoples of the Klamath Tribes so there was no future planning on how to continue through the Winema National Forest."

*Note: This trail is part of the National Recreation Trail #160 I have broken it into sections-Auger (Hager Mountain), Yamsay and Silver Creek. In the future the Forest Service says the segments are going to be changed from assigned numbers (as they currently are) to naming them as one whole trail.

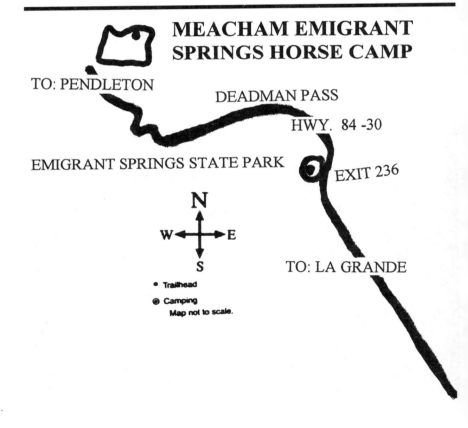

MEACHAM EMIGRANT SPRINGS HORSE CAMP

TO: PENDLETON

DEADMAN PASS

HWY. 84-30

EMIGRANT SPRINGS STATE PARK

EXIT 236

N

W ←→ E

S

TO: LA GRANDE

• Trailhead
⊚ Camping
Map not to scale.

MEACHAM EMIGRANT SPRINGS HORSE CAMP

Oregon State Park, Meacham Emigrant Springs Horse Camp is located off Interstate 84 between the towns of Pendleton and La Grande Oregon. From Pendleton, go southeast passing up and over Deadman Pass and Squaw Creek Overlook. On the east side of the road is the state park. From La Grande go northwest passing the Meacham turnoff to reach Meacham Emigrant Springs Horse Camp. It is well marked from the highway with a picture of a horse on a lead rope on the sign. Camp includes: both "people only camping", and an area for those camping with horses. When you enter, you'll follow the signs to the right and up a hill to reach the horse area. The camps are lettered A-G with 1 corral per site. There are several drive-thru spots and spaces C and D are nice for those needing a side by side camp. The water spigot is at camp D while camps E and F have the big drive-thru. You'll find picnic tables, fire rings, toilets and showers which are down the hill by the "people only" camp. There is a camp wheelbarrow for removal of manure. The setting is grassy under nice shady trees, and is clean. The highway is quite noisy but other than that it is a nice camp for the traveling horse hauler. I found a dirt road north of the camp to ride on to stretch my horse's legs after a long day in the trailer. Some of the sites were in ill-repair but it looked as though it is a work in progress. The fee to stay there when I visited was $14.00 a night. I included this in my book because I know how it is when you are tired and need a place to rest when hauling horses.

Ali waits in her corral

Camp.

JOAQUIN MILLER HORSE CAMP

Joaquin Miller Horse Camp is located off Highway 395 (John Day-Burns Highway). From Burns north to camp it is 20 miles. From John Day south it is around 60 miles. For those of you that travel across Eastern Oregon, you know how open and big it really is. The population is sparse and it is comforting to know that there is a horse camp that you can count on for the night. Joaquin Miller Horse Camp has 15 sites. One site has a set of 4 corrals. There are 6 toilets, 2 hitch rails, and a well with a hand pump. No fee or reservation is required. It is a nice big campground. The setting is under shady pines.

Josie and Doc have a nice ride.

The riding is limited to a few roads, meadows, and some forestland but, when you need a spot to pull over on your way to somewhere else, it is a great place to go. The elevation is at 5600'. I have no detailed map to recommend except the Oregon Road & Recreation Atlas.

For more information contact:
Emigrant Ranger District, 541.573.4300

Camp corrals.

JOAQUIN MILLER
HORSE CAMP

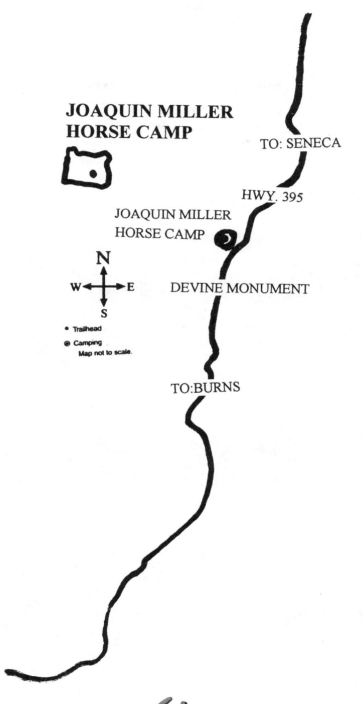

TO: SENECA

HWY. 395

JOAQUIN MILLER
HORSE CAMP

N

W ← → E

S

DEVINE MONUMENT

• Trailhead
⊚ Camping
  Map not to scale.

TO: BURNS

TODD HORSE CAMP

Todd Horse Camp and this section of the Metolius Windigo Trail #99 are located in Central Oregon. I have ridden extensively in the Three Sisters Wilderness. However, I missed riding this small portion of trail somehow. I have included this 9 mile part of the Metolius Windigo Trail #99 to complete the area. For more information and lots of trail miles in the Three Sisters Wilderness, examine my other books; <u>Gone Ridin'</u> and <u>Trail Busters</u>. This trail is open to both mountain bikes and motorcycles as it is just outside of the Three Sisters Wilderness. My friend Terri and I did meet a man on a motorcycle. He was very polite and he yielded the trail to us. In fact he turned off his bike and we chatted awhile. The Forest

Rocky mountain elk.

Three heads are better than one.

On our way to Happy Valley.

Josie & Ali on Metolius Windigo Trail.

THREE SISTERS

WILDERNESS

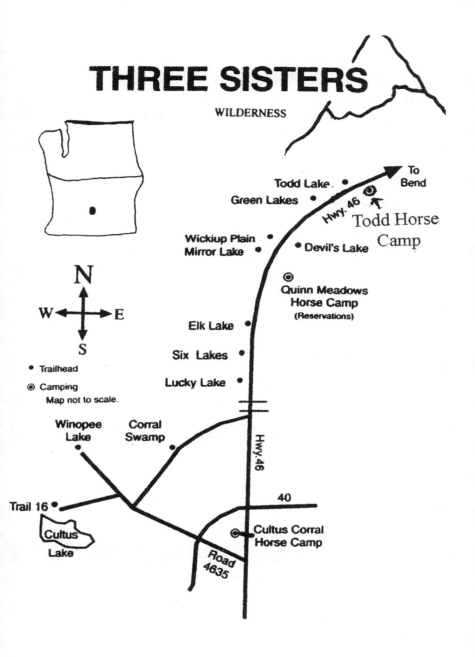

N
W ← → E
S

• Trailhead
◎ Camping
  Map not to scale.

Todd Lake •
Green Lakes •
Hwy. 46

To Bend

Todd Horse Camp

Wickiup Plain •
Mirror Lake •
Devil's Lake •

◎
Quinn Meadows
Horse Camp
(Reservations)

Elk Lake •

Six Lakes •

Lucky Lake •

Winopee
Lake •

Corral
Swamp •

Hwy. 46

40

Trail 16 •

◎ Cultus Corral
Horse Camp

Cultus
Lake

Road
4635

Service indicated that mountain bike travel is heavy on this trail as well. However, we were visiting after Labor Day, and everything, including the campground was pretty vacant.

Directions to Todd Horse Camp: From Bend, drive west on Cascade Lakes Highway 46 for 24 miles. When you reach Todd Lake turnoff, you'll go directly opposite and turn south (left) onto Forest Service Road 4600-390. The little road takes you into camp, which is pretty well hidden behind trees from Highway 46.

Todd Horse Camp includes: There are 6 sites with steel corrals, (one 6-stall, two 4-stall, one 2-stall,) and 2 RV sites (no table or fire ring). There is 1 host site. The elevation is 6000' so, when arriving at a high elevation when your mount is from a lower elevation, be sure to acclimate them before riding them hard. Other amenities include pit toilets, water trough, manure dumps at all sites, day use area, tables and fire pits. The setting is in the trees. The sites are horse users only until 7 P.M., then it is open for public to use. There is no potable water.

For more information contact:

Bend/Fort Rock Ranger District
1230 NE 3rd Suite A262
Bend, Oregon 97701
541.383.4000

Maps to use:
Deschutes National Forest
Three Sisters Wilderness

Metolius Windigo #99

(From Todd Horse Camp to Happy Valley)

Distance: 9 Miles
Altitude: 6000'-6800'
Maps: Deschutes National Forest; Three Sisters Wilderness
Difficulty: Moderate

Connecting Trails: Broken Top Trail and ski trails

Horse Camping: Todd Horse Camp

Trail Description: To begin the Metolius Windigo Trail #99, you'll find the trailhead at the RV section of Todd Horse Camp. It's on the far side of the parking area. Ride south across a bridge, then loop around lava piles, and finally going north. Cross paved Cascade Lakes Highway 46. You'll go directly in to deep timberland. There are two cross-country ski trails that you will pass over. There is a nice view of Broken Top Mountain and meadows here and there. This is a pleasant 9 mile trek to Happy Valley. You'll see blue markers in the trees. These are for winter recreation ski trails. They intersect with Metolius Windigo Trail #99. A mileage sign reads: 5.3 miles to Happy Valley. Follow the horse symbol (there is also a bike symbol) on small posts. So far, the trail has been on an upward trend. It gets a bit steeper, but only for a short distance. More meadows and deep old growth forest await you. Some of the meadows are long valleys with and without water, depending on the time of year. One creek is called Crater Creek Ditch. You will ride through open-aired areas where you'll find fantastic views of Broken Top Mountain, South Sister Mountain, and a red ridge. When the trail goes down a bit there is a sign indicating "Bend Watershed Area". Ride along with more view-points and rolling terrain to an intersection for Broken Top Trail. Continue, still on Metolius Windigo Trail #99. Happy Valley is only 2.5 miles more. You'll see more meadows, go around hillsides, down to cross a creek, and then ford another one. Meander around a hillside, then down gentle and steady to a flatter area along North Fork Tumalo Creek, to meadowland. Then you'll meet up with the Swampy Lakes Trailhead, Trail #23 and Happy Valley. This is a nice long ride and Happy Valley is a "happy" place to eat lunch. There is a good bridge over North Fork Tumalo Creek, and it is easy to water the horses here. If you are going farther north, all the way to Three Creeks Horse Camp, it is another 5 miles. From Todd Horse Camp, the Metolius Windigo Trail #99 also goes south too. For more information, pick up my last book "Trail Busters".

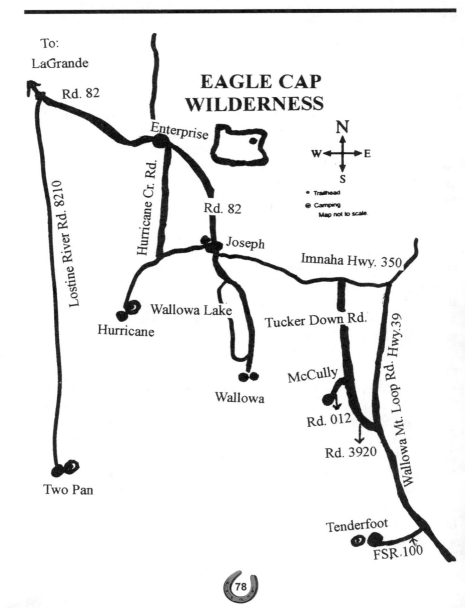

EAGLE CAP WILDERNESS & WALLOWA MOUNTAINS
BY ROBIN OWEN

The Wallowa Mountains in Northeastern Oregon offer some of the best riding in the Northwest. Much more than what is presented here. From relatively easy riding to challenging, the vistas, lakes, rivers and granite peaks are breathtaking. There is usually ample water for stock at creek crossings. For more information on trails and trailheads, check out Hiking Oregon's Eagle Cap Wilderness by Fred Barnard, and Quick Trips to the Wallowas by Louise Rea. Peruse the trail books and maps for rides from the Moss Springs Trailhead.

There are many opportunities for packing in, or point-to-point rides. Much of the Wallowas are in the Eagle Cap Wilderness, and Wilderness rules apply. Check with the Wallowa Whitman Forest Service for up-to-date information on trail conditions, camping availability, fees, etc.. Northwest Parking Passes are required at most trailheads.

Directions to Moss Springs Horse Camp:
Take Highway 237 east of La Grande to Cove. Drive 13 miles more to camp via Mill Creek Road and Forest Service Road 6220 (steep road). Moss Springs Horse Camp is a ways from most of the trails described in this chapter, but it is in the general area. Elevation is 5400'.

Moss Springs Horse Camp includes: There are 12 campsites, 2 star feeders/holding pens; hitching rails, stock water, and a restroom. A parking pass is required and there is a camping fee. Access is to Eagle Cap Wilderness.

There is primitive horse camping along the Lostine River Road, (beyond the National Forest Boundary) at the Tenderfoot Trailhead, and below the Hurricane Ridge Trailhead.

Other Horse Camping:
You can also camp at the fairgrounds in Joseph. Call the Joseph Chamber of Commerce, 541.432.1015, for rates and availability.
The Arrowhead Ranch, near Joseph, offers cabins for you and a place for your horse. For more information, phone 541.426.6420, or check out their website www.arrowheadranchcabins.com.

For more information contact:

Wallowa Whitman Forest Service
8804 Highway 82
Enterprise, OR
541.426.4978

Maps to use:

Wallowa Whitman National Forest
Geo-Graphic's Wallowa Mountains Eagle Cap Wilderness (this map has elevation and trail miles)

Wareen Taylor & Toby, Robin & Rocky-Lostine Valley on the way to Mirror Lake.

Another lake in the Eagle Cap Wilderness.

Ride, Ride, Ride
Color Picture Highlights

Beautiful Crater Lake.

Josie n' Doc in the Potholes Area.

Sue & Willie on a gorgeous fall ride.

Josie and Harley on a crisp autumn outing.

Donna Evans stops for lunch.

Eagle

CJ, Donna J., Robin, Wareen, and John have a great trail ride,

Desert cactus flowers and petrified wood.

Josie and her mare Ali with golden Tamarack trees.

Nice buck.

The Painted Desert on the way to Joaquin Horse Camp.

Josie & Sue stop briefly on their desert ride.

Josie and Harley on the Coal Mines Trail.

Josie riding her mare Breezy.

Josie and Ali on trail near Whitefish Horse Camp.

Mountain goat in the Teanaway.

Josie & Royal found a meadow of Lupine flowers.

Donna and Stormy.

Sandy and Bell, fall foliage.

Josie on Royal.

Blackberries found at Danville Georgetown Trails.

Cowboy Dinner Tree.

Terri and Royal enjoy a stop. Royal passed on in 2009 – R.I.P.

Terri and Charlie riding high above Ellensburg.

Mount Rainier

Josie and Ali on the PCT near Crater Lake.

The beautiful Northwest!

Bonny Lakes

Distance: 6.5 Miles approximately	
Altitude: 6450'-7840'	
Maps: Wallowa Whitman National Forest; Geo-Graphic's Wallowa Mountains Eagle Cap Wilderness	
Difficulty: Moderate	

Directions: From Joseph, drive east on Highway 350 (Imnaha Highway) 8 miles. Turn right on Highway 39 (Wallowa Mountain Loop Road) toward Salt Creek Summit. Continue 13 miles to FSR (Forest Service Road) 100 and turn right. Drive to the end of the road, (about 3 miles) and park.

Horse Camping: There is primitive horse camping available near the Tenderfoot Trailhead with 2 or 3 small sites. There are no amenities or potable water. There is stock water about ¼ mile from the trailhead at Big Sheep Creek.

Trail Description: Start out on Tenderfoot Wagon Road Trail #1819. Cross Big Sheep Creek and travel through a burn area and then open and forested areas. At approximately 1.1 miles, turn right on to East Fork Wallowa Trail #1804 (#1802 depending on your map). The trail follows the Middle Fork of Big Sheep Creek to Bonny Lakes, about 5.5 miles from the turnoff. There are two serene lakes by which to have a leisurely lunch while you take in the beauty of the surrounding mountains.

Robin & Rocky.

Big Sheep Basin.

East Fork Lostine #1662

(To Mirror Lake)

Distance: 7.3 Miles
Altitude: 5584'-7595'
Maps: Wallowa Whitman National Forest; Geo-Graphic's Wallowa Mountains Eagle Cap Wilderness
Difficulty: Moderate-Challenging (rocky and steep terrain in places, side-hills)

Directions: From Lostine on Highway 82, turn south on Lostine River Road 8210 and drive about 17 miles to Two Pan Trailhead at the end of the road. (The first 6 miles are paved, the last 11 miles are gravel). There is ample parking for trucks and trailers to the left and a stock water tank to the north of the parking lot.

Horse Camping: There are 8 sites, with tables, a stock ramp, hitching rails, and a rest room. There is primitive camping along the Lostine River Road once you enter the National Forest. A parking pass is required.

Trail Description: At the junction of trails Minam Lake #1670 and East Fork Lostine #1662, head left on East Fork Lostine Trail #1662. The trail follows the East Fork of Lostine River. There are some large boulders here and there on the trail that my short-legged, but very game horse had a challenge hopping up. The forested trail climbs gradually for 2-3 miles, then climbs steeply before opening to the incredibly beautiful Lostine Valley at 7500' elevation. The trail skirts the west side of the valley before crossing the bridge to the east side of the valley and climbs to Mirror Lake. This is a fragile alpine area and it is important to keep stock on the trail. There are many areas to tie up to, to rest your stock at the lake. Have a leisurely lunch and maybe a short nap if you can give up looking at the lake and the surrounding peaks for a while. Mirror Lake is an entry point to the Lakes Basin.

Pass between Big Sheep Basin and McCully Basin.

East Fork Wallowa #1804
(#1802 depending on your map)

(To Aneroid Lake)

Distance: 6 Miles	
Altitude: 4646'-7500'	
Maps: Wallowa Whitman National Forest; Geo-Graphic's Wallowa Mountains Eagle Cap Wilderness	
Difficulty: Moderate	

Directions: From Joseph, drive to the south end of Wallowa Lake. Turn left at the fork and drive about 1 mile to the end of the road. There is ample parking along the road on the left. The Wallowa Lake Trailhead is to the southeast, behind the powerhouse. Follow the signs to the East Fork Trailhead and East Fork Wallowa Trail #1804 (or #1802, depending on your map). A short way past the trailhead, on the left, is a wide construction trail. Do not take this. There is a loading ramp and hitch rails at this trailhead. A Northwest Parking Pass is not required at Wallowa Trailheads.

Trail Description: The East Fork Wallowa Trail #1804 (#1802) generally follows the East Fork of the Wallowa River, and is forested most of the way. Around 2 miles in, you will come to a dam. At about 5.5 miles, you will come to Roger Lake, (a picturesque stop) before the final climb to Aneroid Lake. Before you arrive at the lake, the trail divides. The right fork is for traffic going up to the lake and the left is for coming down from the lake. This is done because the trails are narrow. It is well signed. There is private property and cabins at the lake, but there are plenty of trees to tie to along the trail while you explore the lake and take in the views with lunch. Elevation at Aneroid Lake is 7500'. This trail has some rocky terrain, is steep in places, and has some steep side hills.

*Note: The Geo-Graphic's map shows East Fork Wallowa Trail as #1802, and the Wallowa Whitman National Forest Map reads #1804.

Hurricane Creek #1807

Distance: 10.1 Miles	
Altitude: 5026'-7440'	
Maps: Wallowa Whitman National Forest; Geo-Graphic's Wallowa Mountains Eagle Cap Wilderness	
Difficulty: Moderate	

Directions: From Enterprise, on Highway 82, turn south on Hurricane Creek Road. Follow for a bit over 5 miles to the Grange Hall. Airport Road to the left continues to Joseph. The graveled road to the right goes to Hurricane Creek Trailhead, approximately 4 miles.

Horse Camping: There is ample parking for trucks and trailers, a loading ramp, and a rest room. There is primitive camping below the trailhead. A Northwest Parking Pass is required at this trailhead.

Connecting Trails: Falls Creek, Legore Lake, and Echo Lake

Trail Description: The Hurricane Creek Trail #1807 is one of the entry points to the Lakes Basin. It is a lovely and interesting trail to ride for however far you wish to go. It also provides access to the trails to Falls Creek, Legore Lake and Echo Lake. Check with the Forest Service for conditions before attempting these very strenuous and steep climbs. Also check to see if they are open to stock. At about 3 miles, just before reaching Slick Rock Creek, you will come to a spectacular gorge. The stock trail is to the right, before the gorge (the trail along the gorge is precarious-we missed the "inland" trail the first time up and got off to lead our horses, heart in mouth). Find a place to tie up below the trail just before the gorge and go take a look. It is awesome.

Headwaters of the Minam River, south end of Minam Lake.

The trail from the pass down to McCully Basin

Ice Lake #1808

Distance: 7.9 Miles	
Altitude: 4646'-7920'	
Maps: Wallowa Whitman National Forest; Geo-Graphic's Wallowa Mountains Eagle Cap Wilderness	
Difficulty: Moderate-Challenging (rocky terrain, steep in places, steep side-hills, and drop-offs)	

Directions: Start this ride from the Wallowa Lake Trailhead. From Enterprise, take State Highway 82 through Joseph and go past Wallowa Lake. The trailhead is at the end of the road approximately 1 mile past the lake. Parking is available at the trailhead along with a loading ramp and hitch rails for stock. A parking pass is not required at Wallowa Trailheads.

Trail Description: From the Wallowa Lake Trailhead, follow the signs to the West Fork Trailhead, West Fork Wallowa Trail #1820. Ride along the east side of the West Fork of the Wallowa River for 2.8 miles until you reach the turnoff to Ice Lake Trail #1808, to the right. The trail crosses the river, and then starts to climb, very steeply in places, for 5.1 miles to Ice Lake, which is at approximately 8000' elevation. Along the way the trail looks over a gorge, with views of a waterfall in the distance. The corners of a few of the switchbacks are close to the drop-off to the gorge. Ice Lake is the main base camp for climbing nearby peaks. The views of the Matterhorn and Craig Mountain are spectacular. On the way, look for mountain sheep on the Hurwal Divide to the right, and on the peaks surrounding the lake.

I've got quite an itch!

Kid goat.

Minam Lake #1670

Distance: 6 Miles	
Altitude: 5606'-7373'	
Maps: Wallowa Whitman National Forest; Geo-Graphic's Wallowa Mountains Eagle Cap Wilderness	
Difficulty: Moderate	

Directions: From Lostine on Highway 82, turn south on Lostine River Road 8210 and drive about 17 miles to Two Pan Trailhead at the end of the road. (The first 6 miles are paved, the last 11 miles are gravel). There is ample parking for trucks and trailers to the left and a stock water tank to the north of the parking lot.

Horse Camping: There are 8 sites, with tables, a stock ramp, hitching rails, and a rest room. There is primitive camping along the Lostine River Road once you enter the National Forest. A parking pass is required.

Connecting Trail: 1662

Trail Description: Minam Lake Trail #1670, starts at the message board and registration station. At the fork of Trails Minam Lake #1670 and East Fork Lostine Trail #1662, (a short distance from the trailhead) head left on Minam Lake Trail #1670. The trail follows the Lostine River and is mostly forested with occasional open meadows. There are many lunch spots around Minam Lake. Take the time to go to the south end of the lake to see the headwaters of the long Minam River.

Minam Lake.

Robin & Toby at Minam lake.

Tenderfoot Trailhead to McCully Creek Trailhead (point-to-point)

(Tenderfoot Wagon Road Trail #1819 and McCully Creek Trail #1812)

Distance: 10.5 Miles

Altitude: 6450'-8650'

Maps: Wallowa Whitman National Forest; Geo-Graphic's Wallowa Mountains Eagle Cap Wilderness

Difficulty: Moderate-Challenging (Steep side-hills and terrain, trail finding skills)

Directions: From Joseph, drive east on Highway 350 (Imnaha Highway) 8 miles. Turn right on Highway 39 (Wallowa Mountain Loop Road) toward Salt Creek Summit. Continue 13 miles to FSR (Forest Service Road) 100 and turn right. Drive to the end of the road, (about 3 miles) and park. There is primitive horse camping available near the Tenderfoot Trailhead, with 2 or 3 small sites, but no amenities or potable water. There is stock water about ¼ mile from the trailhead at Big Sheep Creek. To leave a rig at McCully Creek Trailhead, drive about 5 ½ miles east from Joseph on the Imnaha Highway (Hwy 350). Turn right (south) on Tucker Down Road (County Road 633), and drive about 4½ miles to FSR 012 and turn right. There is ample room for trailer parking, a hitch rail, loading ramp and a rest room. There is no camping available.

Trail Description: The trail from Tenderfoot starts at the northwest corner of the parking area. Follow Tenderfoot Wagon Road Trail #1819 about ¼ mile to cross Big Sheep Creek. Continue on through a burn area and open and partly forested side-hills. At the junction of McCully Creek Trail #1812, turn right toward McCully Creek Basin. The trail winds up and up through forest and meadows, until you reach Big Sheep Basin. The trail essentially disappears at this point. Ride into the basin and generally head toward the northeast corner. Soon you will note rock cairns (piled rocks) that mark the trail up the last steep ascent to the pass between Big Sheep Basin and McCully Basin. At each cairn, scan the terrain until you see the next one. Ride to it and scan again. The last steep haul to the pass switchbacks up to the top. The trail is narrow and the side-hill is steep. The horses will need frequent rest stops to catch their breath as the elevation is high. The pass elevation is 8700'. Take a few moments at the top to appreciate the fantastic views of the Wallowa Mountains to the west and south, and the beautiful Wallowa Valley to the north. The trail down to McCully Basin is also steep, but once you get to the basin, the trail flattens out, and then drops gradually, following McCully Creek. The trail from McCully Basin to the McCully Trailhead is moderate to easy. If a point-to-point ride isn't possible, the rides to and from Big Sheep Basin and McCully Creek Basin are wonderful too.

COWGIRLS AND MAPS

 While visiting the Mount Adams Horse Camp, which is on the south side of Mount Adams, my friend Terri and I met some gals that make maps for horse enthusiasts. They were on a research mission mapping the area. One of them had an unfortunate accident while going around a downed tree on the trail. The horse made it around okay, but the rider ended up with a nasty puncture-cut in her leg from a limb of the tree. Being a hearty bunch of cowgirls, they had gone to the hospital, fixed up the leg and were back in camp again. They went out riding the following day, which was about the time we arrived. We saw them come into camp and one gal was limping pretty badly. We got to chatting and they told us their story. We had several nice meals with them and watched as they dressed the injury in the glow of the fire. This was not a small wound! On the far side of camp there was a lone camper with no horse. Her aim was to hike up Mount Adam's south slope. She also happened to be a doctor. She volunteered her services to help to clean and dress the leg. It was quite the ordeal as she scrubbed, wiped, smeared medicine on it, and finally wrapping it, only to do it all over again in the morning. My riding buddy is a pharmacist. She was helpful in counseling them on which drugs to use, the correct dosages, and frequency the medicine was to be taken for the best results. These tough gals had even video-taped the hospital procedure and we all watched the film on their lap top. Nobody here possesses a weak stomach. They finally decided there was no reason to stay and risk getting the wound dirty. The rider would be more comfortable at home anyway. They packed up and left the next day. The gal that was hurt had a doctor appointment in two days anyhow. The camp doctor thought that was a wise decision. They only cut their stay short by a day. It was very interesting and makes you want to check your basic first aid kit. It is a good idea to update and include a wide assortment of essentials. I traded them trail books for trail maps. – Josie

John on Ruby, McCully Creek Trail.

McCully Trailhead.

West Fork Wallowa #1820

(To Frazier Lake)

Distance: 9 Miles approximately	
Altitude: 4645'-7127'	
Maps: Wallowa Whitman National Forest; Geo-Graphic's Wallowa Mountains Eagle Cap Wilderness	
Difficulty: Moderate	

Directions: From Joseph, drive to the south end of Wallowa Lake. Turn left at the fork and drive about 1 mile to the end of the road. There is ample parking along the road on the left. The Wallowa Lake Trailhead is to the southeast, behind the powerhouse. Follow the signs to the West Fork Trailhead and West Fork Wallowa Trail #1820. There is a loading ramp and hitch rails at this trailhead. A Northwest Parking Pass is not required at Wallowa Trailheads.

Trail Description: West Fork Wallowa Trail #1820 follows the West Fork of the Wallowa River. A good place for a break is Six Mile Meadow. Only 3 miles more to go. The trail mostly climbs gradually, but it is a long way to the lake. If you want to stay over, there are some good camping spots. Check with the Forest Service for regulations and availability. When we got there, we met a group who had been dropped off by a packer and had stayed several days. They were amazed that we rode both ways in one day. I replied that I wouldn't be sorry when I got off of my horse back at the trailhead! The lake is beautiful, with many lunch spots to choose from.

Wallowa Lake.

Doe, a deer.

DANVILLE GEORGETOWN EQUESTRIAN PARK

By Donna Joncas & Josie Rusho

Danville Georgetown is a designated "Open Space" that features more than 25 miles of well-maintained trails. The square mileage is small, about 800 acres, but it is interlaced with criss-crossing trails. Most of the Danville Georgetown site is owned by King County and trails are maintained with the help of The Washington Backcountry Horsemen (Maple Valley Chapter). The name "Danville" comes from the old railroad line that used to travel through the north section of this region, and the name "Georgetown" comes from the old mining town, which is now merged with Ravensdale. This refers to the southern section. The Seattle Public Utilities Pipeline supplies water for Seattle from the watershed area at Taylor Mountain, which is just up the road. Trails off the Pipeline Road are fairly good most of the year and not too wet. Depending on the weather, though, some of the trails off the SE Summit-Landsburg Road across from the junior high school can be wet and slippery-particularly the Lone Wolf Trail. The wettest time of year is early spring through June. The trails' elevation ranges from 500'-700'. All of the paths are rated in the "Moderate" scope of difficulty. There is no camping in the areas and no facilities. No parking permit is required. The majority of the terrain is rolling, with dense foliage, trees with moss, blackberry bushes and ferns. The footing on the school side of the road is rockier than the other side, which is soft and nice. (Probably because it is closer to the Cedar River bed.) There are limited views. However the riding is pleasant and the groomed trails are a delight to ride. It is a shady place to escape to on a hot sunny day. There was some bear scat on the trail but luckily we saw no bears. Other animal life include: bobcat, elk, owls, beaver, rabbits, red-tailed hawks, woodpeckers, quail, and salamanders. I loved the long green ferns and the earthy smells. There are over 30 different varieties of moss and some even bloom! We did not bring "Daisy" the trail dog along because of the limited visibility on the road crossings. We had a blast riding here. First, we rode the trails on one side of the road. Then we came back to the rig, tied the horses to the trailer, and sat in the camper to eat our lunch. After lunch we proceeded to do the

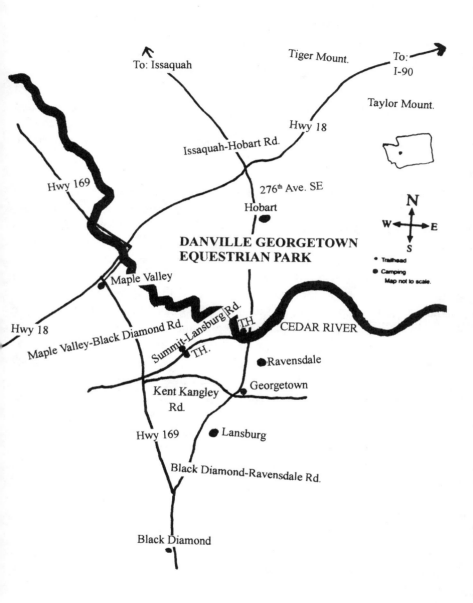

To: Issaquah

Tiger Mount.

To: I-90

Taylor Mount.

Hwy 18

Issaquah-Hobart Rd.

Hwy 169

276th Ave. SE

Hobart

DANVILLE GEORGETOWN EQUESTRIAN PARK

N

W ←→ E

S

• Trailhead

● Camping

Map not to scale.

Maple Valley

Hwy 18

Maple Valley-Black Diamond Rd.

Summit-Lansburg Rd.

T.H.

CEDAR RIVER

T.H.

Ravensdale

Kent Kangley Rd.

Georgetown

Hwy 169

Lansburg

Black Diamond-Ravensdale Rd.

Black Diamond

other half of the trail system, on the opposite side of the road. We did not do every one, but felt we got a good sample of the trails. One area on the south side of the road is an old Indian trail. Some of the trails on the north side have breathtaking views of the Cedar River. Donna J. used to live down the road from here and has been on just about every trail. We found one trail that was not listed on the map. We figured it must be a newer one. It is called "Porcupine Pie", and is located off of the Ridge Trail. Almost all of the trail intersections were marked. It is wise to always bring a map anyway and count the turns. The trails have been divided into which side of the road they are on so it will be easier to read with the map in hand. There are 8 trails on each side of the road.

Directions to Danville Georgetown Equestrian Park: The Danville Georgetown Trails are easy to find. *If coming from the north:* from I-90, go south on Highway 18 for 6 ½ miles. Take the Hobart Exit, to Issaquah-Hobart Road. Turn left going under Highway 18-Issaquah-Hobart becomes 276th, Ave. SE. Go south for about 4 ½ miles. If coming from the Auburn direction on Highway 18, take the Hobart Exit. Turn right and go south about 4 ½ miles on 276th Ave. SE. Just past the Cedar River Bridge on the right, just before Summit-Landsburg Road, is roadside parking. Please do not block the access gate for the pipeline road. The parking is more limited at this trailhead than the one by the school. Refer to the map and read on. There is another roadside parking area that is a short 1½ miles from this one. Reach it by turning right onto Summit-Lansburg Road. Continue driving west on the same road past the stop sign until you pass the Tahoma Junior High School on the right. Just past the school you'll find the trailheads for Old Indian, 3 Elk, and Putnam Trails. There is a homemade sign, and a road sign that reads "Horse Crossing". There is ample room to park in the gravel alongside the road. It stretches ½ mile, so any size rig can fit.

If coming from the west: from State Route 169 (Maple Valley-Black Diamond Road) you'll turn east and onto Kent-Kangley Road. Turn left onto Summit-Landsburg Road. Watch for the homemade trail signs and "Horse crossing" signs on the right, about ½ mile after turning on to the Landsburg Road. There is ample room to park in the gravel alongside the road. It stretches ½ mile, so any size rig can fit. Limited parking is also available off the Issaquah-Hobart Road (276th Ave. SE). Read above directions and refer to the map. There are no facilities at these trailheads.

Maps to use: Hand-out type maps for this area are located down the Pipeline Road. Look for information on the web at http://www.frcv.org/?id=54 under Draft Danville Georgetown Equestrian Park. The web site location shows you all of the trails and their names. CowboyMaps.com also carries a map for the area, for a fee.

Donna J. and Penny make their way up the Ridge Trail.

South side of the trail-system "Georgetown Trails at Danville"

Barn Owl

Distance: Short, under ½ mile	
Altitude: 700'	
Maps: Danville Georgetown Equestrian Park; Hand-out type near trails; CowboyMaps.com	
Difficulty: Moderate	

Directions: This trail has no trailhead

Connecting Trails: Ridge Loop and Three Elk

Trail Description: This trail is short and connects the Ridge Loop Trail to Three Elk Trail. It is on the far south edge of the Danville Georgetown Equestrian Park.

Berry Bear

Distance: .5 Mile approximately

Altitude: 650'-700'

Maps: Danville Georgetown Equestrian Park; Hand-out type near trails; CowboyMaps.com

Difficulty: Moderate

Directions: This trail has no trailhead

Connecting Trails: Ridge Loop, and Three Elk

Trail Description: This trail is in dense forest for the whole length and connects two major trails, Three Elk Trail and Ridge Loop. Loops are possible.

THAT 0-8

The worst year that 0-8,
Mare named "Ali" up and died,
Left me in a horrible state,
The tears welled like a tide,
No blame, no shame, just fate!

Looking for trail horses, far and wide,
Got a mare, stolen outta my gate,
A gelding, wanted to bite my hide,
The snow's a melting, it's getting late,
Just looking for a horse to ride!

– Josie

WHERE DID MY HORSE "BREEZY" GO?

In the spring of 2008 after my mare "Ali" died, I had a dream of a white mare with a black forelock. In June of 2008 a similarly marked horse I called "Breezy"came to me by way of an acquaintance. She was a nice mare, 9 years old, although not at all seasoned for trail riding. She also had sensitive feet. My farrier and I thought it was a problem that a little tender loving care could fix. We worked on re-shaping her feet and she got somewhat better. I had all of her shots updated, had a masseuse work on some sore poll muscles, had her teeth floated and put her on some good vitamins and supplements for her feet. She was okay to ride, and her feet became a lot better, but she was still quite green-broke for the places I like to go. I was selective on the trails I rode, so I wouldn't overload her brain and body and make her sour or scare her. That August I took her to Oregon on a 10-day trip. When I brought her back, I put her on pasture. I noticed that it was the pasture grass that was affecting her feet after she became somewhat tender-footed again. I put her on dry-lot and let her out on grass only a little at a time. She was better in no time, and was never lame so I continually rode her. One Thursday I got a call from her previous owner we'll call "Lily". She missed the horse and wanted to buy her back. Even though I had a lot of time and energy (not to mention money) invested in "Breezy", I felt sorry for "Lily" as she had raised the mare. I told her the mare's chronic tender foot problem had not improved as much as I had hoped, and it would be okay if she bought her back. We agreed on a price, and set a date for the up-coming Sunday for "Lily" to pick her up. On Friday I went riding on one of my geldings and when I returned home the mare's pen was empty! I figured that "Lily" had something to do with it. I looked around for an envelope for payment. Nope, not a thing. I went in the house and found that "Lily" had left a message on my phone telling me she and a friend had taken the mare. I called "Lily" back, to no avail. About 7:00 P.M. I went to her house with my horse trailer and found that "Breezy" was not there. **Had she stolen "Breezy", then hidden her somewhere?** "Lily" came out of her house and told me she was taking my horse to the vet the following day to have her feet looked at and she would deduct the price of the vet call from the amount we discussed for the buy-back fee. I told Lily, "It is not your horse until you pay me, then you can do whatever you want to with her." She dared me to call the Sheriff, so I did. Enough said. Lickity-split she came up with the cash in less than an hour. She should thank her lucky stars that I did not press charges, and have her arrested. The Sheriff informed me that if she was convicted she would be faced with at least **one felony.** She may have lost her job as a nurse and ended up with a criminal record! I am not regretful that I owned "Breezy" because she helped me heal the wound of losing my mare "Ali". I hold no grudge toward "Lily". However, let this be a lesson-if you sell a horse-it is a final sale. The horse is not yours until you buy it back following a mutual agreement with the rightful owner, regardless of your "feelings".

– Josie

Lone Wolf

Distance: ¾ Mile approximately

Altitude: 650' -700'

Maps: Danville Georgetown Equestrian Park; Hand-out type near trails; CowboyMaps.com

Difficulty: Moderate

Directions: This trail has no trailhead.

Connecting Trails: Three Elk and Ridge Loop

Trail Description: Lone Wolf Trail slices the Ridge Loop in half. All in woodland, deep and mysterious.

Old Indian

Distance: ¾ Mile

Altitude: 600' Flat

Maps: Danville Georgetown Equestrian Park; Hand-out type near trails; CowboyMaps.com

Difficulty: Moderate

Directions: Begin this ride from the traillhead on the west side of the junior high school Three Elk Trail also begins from this point. Across the street is Coyote and the west end of Putnam Loop Trails.

Connecting Trails: Three Elk, Squeaky Mouse Road, and Putnam Loop Trail

Trail Description: Old Indian Trail runs parallel with the Summit Lansburg Road. There is a hand-written sign that reads: "The earliest maps of this area, late 1800's, show a major transportation route for Native Americans in this location. The trail went from Puget Sound to Rattlesnake Prairie (now Rattlesnake Lake)." The path is about 200 years old and has access to several trails for loop possibilities. It is a nice level trail with good footing for the horses.

Porcupine Pie

Distance: ½ Mile approximately
Altitude: 700' about
Maps: Danville Georgetown Equestrian Park; Hand-out type near trails; CowboyMaps.com
Difficulty: Moderate

Directions: This trail has no trailhead

Connecting Trails: Ridge Loop and Squeaky Mouse Road

Trail Description: This is a newer trail and looks like it is very short. It is located at the east end of the Danville Georgetown Equestrian Park. We did not ride this one yet.

Putnam Loop

Distance: ¾ Mile for this side of the road
Altitude: 600' Flat
Maps: Danville Georgetown Equestrian Park; Hand-out type near trails; CowboyMaps.com
Difficulty: Moderate

Directions: This Putnam Loop Trail begins directly across the street from the junior high. There is access at a trailhead on the east edge of the park's trail system off of a small road.

Connecting Trail: Ridge Loop

Trail Description: It loops around, including both sides of Lansburg Road. Total mileage for this trail is about 3-4 miles. On this side of the road the trail parallels Landsburg Road and heads east and west. It links up with the Pipeline near Cedar River on the north side of the trail system.

Ridge Loop

Distance: 3-4 Miles	
Altitude: 600'-700'	
Maps: Danville Georgetown Equestrian Park; Hand-out type near trails; CowboyMaps.com	
Difficulty: Moderate	

Directions: This trail has no trailhead

Connecting Trails: Three Elk, Berry Bear, Lone Wolf, Porcupine Pie, Squeaky Mouse Road, and Barn Owl

Trail Description: We enjoyed this trail. It was deep and wooded. It had several spots that had gravel brought in to what looked like could otherwise be soggy bottom areas. It rises to a small ridge and crosses numerous trails. It has one switchback on the upper end and it is well placed. The ridge part of the ride is at the far south portion of the park. If you don't do any other one of these trails, we recommend this one for a sample of the area's rides. As with all of the trails, the footing is wonderful. Hardly a rock anywhere.

Squeaky Mouse Road

Distance: ¾ Mile approximately	
Altitude: 650'-700'	
Maps: Danville Georgetown Equestrian Park; Hand-out type near trails; CowboyMaps.com	
Difficulty: Moderate	

Directions: No real trailhead

Connecting Trails: Ridge Loop and Old Indian

Trail Description: We have not ridden this whole trail yet. It parallels the Landsburg Road, going east and west, basically.

Three Elk

Distance: 1 Mile approximately
Altitude: 600'-700'
Maps: Danville Georgetown Equestrian Park; Hand-out type near trails; CowboyMaps.com
Difficulty: Moderate

Directions: This trail starts at the same trailhead as Old Indian Trail, just west of the junior high school. Across the street is Coyote and the west end of Putnam Loop Trails.

Connecting Trails: Ridge Loop, Berry Bear, Lone Wolf, and Barn Owl

Trail Description: Three Elk Trail cuts the Ridge Trail in half and can be used in loops. It too is all wooded and has big mossy timberland and ferns. These trails make you feel like you are in a rain forest. We visited when the weather was overcast-not too hot, and not too cold. It was perfect. We drove over for the day from eastern Washington and it was late in July.

Big Eared Bat

Distance: ¼ Mile	
Altitude: 600' Flat	
Maps: Danville Georgetown Equestrian Park; Hand-out type near trails; CowboyMaps.com	
Difficulty: Moderate	

Directions: This trail has no trailhead.

Connecting Trails: Putnam Loop and Coyote

Trail Description: Big Eared Bat Trail is one of the shortest trails and is all wooded. It is used in connecting trails for possible loops.

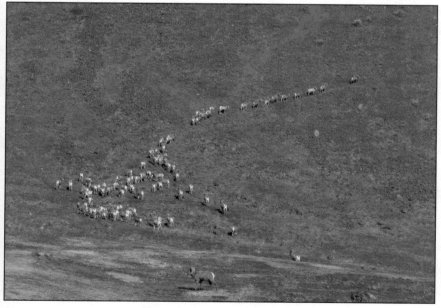

Sheep leaving from the valley.

Coyote

Distance: ¼ Mile approximately

Altitude: 600'

Maps: Danville Georgetown Equestrian Park; Hand-out type near trails; CowboyMaps.com

Difficulty: Moderate

Directions: This trail starts at the same trailhead as the west end of Putnam Loop Trail, just west of the junior high school. Across the street is Old Indian and Three Elk Trails.

Connecting Trails: Putnam Loop, Big Eared Bat, Tilly, and Raccoon

Trail Description: Coyote Trail is a trail that is used to access a web of other trails. We got mixed up a couple of times and enjoyed the chaos. Ya gotta laugh out loud! It is located on the west side of the school.

Mountain Beaver

Distance: ¼ Mile approximately

Altitude: 600'

Maps: Danville Georgetown Equestrian Park; Hand-out type near trails; CowboyMaps.com

Difficulty: Moderate

Directions: This trail starts just west of the junior high school, at the edge of the school boundary.

Connecting Trail: Putnam Loop

Trail Description: Mountain Beaver Trail is a very short trail and runs along the west edge of the school. It is used to connect to Putnam Loop Trail.

Pipeline

Distance: 3 Miles of it are close to the Danville Georgetown Trail System	
Altitude: 500'	
Maps: Danville Georgetown Equestrian Park; Hand-out type near trails; CowboyMaps.com	
Difficulty: Moderate	

Directions: Just past the Cedar River Bridge on the corner by 276th Ave. SE (Hobart-Issaquah Road) is roadside parking. <u>Please do not block the access gate for the pipeline road.</u> The parking is more limited at this trailhead than the area by the school. See the map for more information.

Connecting Trails: Putnam Loop and Skunk

Trail Description: On the west end of the Pipeline Road is a trail on the right that connects with the Cedar River Trail on the north side of the river. You can make a loop back to your trailer if you are parked at Lansburg. (The Cedar River Trail runs from Landsburg to Renton.) It is an old railroad bed with good footing and has a few trestle crossings along the way. Turn left off the pipeline and you can access the west end of Putnam Loop. All trails along the Cedar River that go off to the right go to private property or private roads for local access.

Mountain goat and her twins, again!

Putnam Loop

Distance: 4½ Miles for this side of the road	
Altitude: 500'-600'	
Maps: Danville Georgetown Equestrian Park; Hand-out type near trails; CowboyMaps.com	
Difficulty: Moderate	

Directions: There are several access areas. One way is to go down the Pipeline Trail about ½ mile and you will see a sign with a map of the area. The Putnam Trail takes off to the right. Another way is just east of the junior high school. The parking is not good here. Putnam Trail is across the street.

Connecting Trails: Pipeline, Skunk, Mountain Beaver, Coyote, Raccoon, Big Eared Bat, and Tilly

Trail Description: Starting from the Landsburg area by the Cedar River, go down the Pipeline Trail for about ½ mile and you will see a sign with a map of the area. The Putnam Trail takes off to the right. The Putnam Trail leaves the Pipeline and follows the Cedar River for about 1 mile. Along the river there are big river rocks in places, but most of the trail is very nice. Follow the trail on the map. You will see how it comes out and onto the Pipeline Trail in two different places. It then goes to the right down the Pipeline Trail, continuing again on the left side of the Pipeline Trail. It ends here up on the Landsburg Road, east of the junior high school. Many trails take off from the Putnam Trail between the Pipeline Trail and the Landsburg Road and a number of loops can be made. All trails along the Cedar River that go off to the right go to private property or private roads for local access.

Rocky Mountain big horn sheep – ram.

Raccoon

Distance: ½ Mile approximately

Altitude: 600'

Maps: Danville Georgetown Equestrian Park; Hand-out type near trails; CowboyMaps.com

Difficulty: Moderate

Directions: This trail has no trailhead

Connecting Trails: Putnam Loop, Coyote, and Tilly

Trail Description: Raccoon Trail is a fun little trail that runs beside a gully. We enjoyed this one. The trails on this side of the road have a slant down toward the Pipeline Access. Near the school they are more level.

Skunk

Distance: ½ Mile approximately

Altitude: 500'

Maps: Danville Georgetown Equestrian Park; Hand-out type near trails; CowboyMaps.com

Difficulty: Moderate

Directions: This trail has no trailhead

Connecting Trails: Putnam Loop and Pipeline Trail

Trail Description: Skunk Trail connects the far eastern side of the park's trails together.

Tilly

Distance: ½ Mile approximately

Altitude: 600'

Maps: Danville Georgetown Equestrian Park; Hand-out type near trails; CowboyMaps.com

Difficulty: Moderate

Directions: This trail has no trailhead.

Connecting Trails: Coyote and Putnam Loop

Trail Description: Tilly Trail is a nice forested path. A lot of the trails are part old road and part single track trail. It is located on the west end of the trail system.

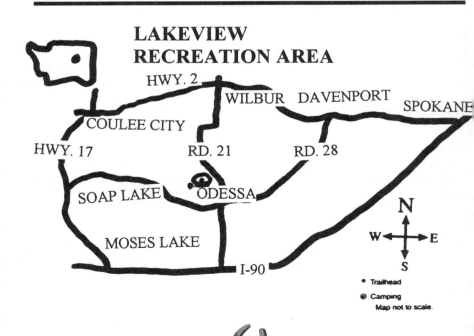

LAKEVIEW RECREATION AREA
(Ranch House Horse Camp)

Lakeview Recreation Area is located in north-central Washington. The closest town is Odessa, 7 miles south of the Ranch House Horse Camp. It is approximately 120 miles from Ellensburg via I-90, and about 90 miles from Spokane via I-90 (75 miles driving on Highway 28/US2). The big lakes shown on the BLM pamphlet are called Pacific Lake and Walter Lake. Unfortunately the water has been drained, due to irrigation. Remnants of the lake include a white line etched in rocks, and a deep depression where the lake once stood. The surrounding region is filled with small undisturbed lakes. Tall, green grasses with birds and deer inhabit the wetland oasis. This land exhibits evidence of the great Missoula Flood event that occurred over 12,500 years ago. The deep rocky Lake Creek Canyon has sprawling views of land, which has been pushed and eroded. Left in the wake are stones of worn and marred Columbia River Basalt rock, bare of surface soil. Remaining are geological formations of pothole lakes, ravines, and saturated meadowland. The wheat fields around the area were not stricken by the fury of floodwaters. Rolling hillsides and prairie are seemingly endless as you ride your horse. There are wildflowers, sagebrush and grasslands. I was surprised at the nice footing for the horses-soft with few rocks. Do watch for holes. You can pretend you are an old-time rancher going out to check the fence line for repairs. I love to go riding where my imagination is stimulated and runs free. The wild west has a certain charm and a special place in my heart. Five of us gals went and we had a great visit. The Ranch House Horse Camp is rather nice and is quiet. There is an abundant variety of wildlife in the area. We listened to the night birds-haunting hoots from the owls, and screeching night hawks. An array of

Corrals at camp.

Loading chute at camp.

day-shift birds kept vigil on us too from their perches high in the limbs and nests. They sing lovely tunes. The coyotes' stark howls startled us at dusk. We felt they were close. We kept a sharp eye for rattlers, although we only saw a bull snake. Stray bunnies, jack rabbits, short-horned lizards, ducks, killdeer (bird), mule deer and strange beetles were seen in camp and on the trails. The BLM information lists other wildlife such as: Sage-grouse, American White Pelican, Painted Turtles and Tiger Salamanders as well as badger. We visited in July and it was scorching hot by noon, so our rides were early morning and evening events. Several of us had inexperienced horses that were rookies on trails. It is a great place to build confidence for both rider and horse. There is room to roam and explore in this region. The main trail goes from the Ranch House Horse Camp to the town of Odessa. The trail is over 12 miles long. Part of the trail is road and part is trail. There are several loops from camp on "Off Road Vehicle" (ORV) trails as well. Be sure to stay on the Bureau of Land Management (BLM) lands (marked in tan coloring on the BLM map). Other lands are "Private or Other"-respect these restrictions. We want to keep these riding options open by obeying the regulations. Some maps show the trail system

outside of the BLM area. However, if they are private you do need the permission of the land owner to tread on his or her property. Endurance races have been held here. I'm sure they obtained special permission to use these adjacent lands for the course they set up. It is not a "given" that you can ride the same course. I highly suggest that you use and

Laurie and Rocky find a nice meadow while riding the off road vehicle loop.

compare maps. We met the BLM worker that lives with his dog across

Ranch House Horse Camp.

the street from the Ranch House Horse Camp. He shared his insight and information about the area. He told us that the ranch is not a homestead, but an old cattle operation. After that the ranch was used to house wild horses, brought up from the Burns area in Oregon. They were sold at this site. That explained why the corrals are so tight and high. The wooden panels are so close together that you can hardly see in. He explained that the wild horses need a corral that they can't see out of. The wildest ones will try to escape if they can see through the smallest crack. There were black tarps strapped to the tops of the gates and draping down for the same reason. The original pen was for cattle, and is the outside wooden structure of the corral. We all had a lot of fun. When it got real hot we drug out feed buckets and "muck" buckets, filled them with cool water and soaked our hot feet. We sipped our cold beverages and chatted all afternoon. We even had popsicles. As the sun dipped and the evening breeze strolled into camp, we settled in for the night. I hope you take time off and come experience the desert. If you love that "Old West" feeling I think you will enjoy Lakeview Recreation Area as much as we did.

Directions to Ranch House Horse Camp:
Drive on I-90 to Highway 21, Odessa Exit (206). Drive north on Highway 21 for 19 miles. It has a slight jog, but it is well signed. Drive through the town of Odessa. Still on Highway 21, go north out of town 2 miles. Turn left onto Lakeview Ranch Road-it is gravel. Go 5 miles. The Ranch House Horse Camp is on the left and is signed. From Spokane allow 1-2 hours, from Ellensburg about 3 hours travel time.

Ranch House Horse Camp includes:
There is room for any size rig, with ample parking in a big circle. An extra parking area is behind the ranch outbuildings by the trailhead, and possibly to the north of the corrals. Call ahead if you have a big group

Unique corrals at camp.

Old wagon.

ride. There are 5 big stout, spacious, high wooden pens. One of the pens could be made into 2 easily. In fact we saw the metal panels sitting aside that look like that is just what they are used for. There is water for "horses only" with a sign indicating that the water has nitrates in it. There is a short hose connected to the water spigot. We brought extra hoses so we could easily reach the watering troughs in each pen. Some of the troughs are set up so 2 pens share 1 trough. Call ahead to make sure the water is available. The manure pile is to the north of the pens. The BLM man offered a wheel barrow, but we had brought one of our own of course. There are 2 picnic tables, 1 fire pit, trash service, and overhead light for the outbuildings. There is room for at least 5 rigs in the circle, although not enough width to pass each other. There is grass in the middle of the circle, and another spigot-also NOT POTABLE. The nice green lawn made for a clean camp, tent, or camper. The elm trees are huge and shady when the sun gets hot. One chemical toilet is normally available at the site from May through September. There is also a permanent vault outhouse at the Pacific Lake picnic site less than one mile away that is open all year. Over by the corrals there is a loading chute and a place set up to sign-in and tell about your visit. We found that interesting. There also is a place with the maps for the area and they are free! Camp is at 1595' elevation.

For more information contact:

Spokane District
Bureau of Land Management
1103 North Fancher Road
Spokane, WA 99212-1275
509-536-1200
www.or.blm.gov/spokane

Maps to use:
Lakeview Recreation Area
Washington Road & Recreation Atlas

Crater and Three lakes

Distance: 2 Miles approximately
Altitude: 1595'-1602' about
Maps: BLM and Washington Road & Recreation Atlas
Difficulty: Moderate

Directions: Take the trail west from camp signed "Trail"

Connecting Trails: Cross Country Shortcut, and Odessa Lake Creek

Trail Description: Starting from Ranch House Horse Camp, go between the outbuildings to the west and you'll see the trail. Follow the trail, which starts as a 2-track road. It leads through grasslands and as it comes closer to the first lake it weaves in between some hills. It is a natural draw. When the road quits, follow the path up a short rocky section of trail and you'll see the first of three lakes. It is amazingly beautiful in here. Follow the shoreline above the lake on good tread to another lake on the left. This area is known as Lakeview Ranch Crater. There is tall grasslands and wetlands with water fowl. We saw many ducks. At the third lake you'll follow the trail on the right side (north shoreline). This one has a cute island in it. The trail becomes a 2-track again in tall sage and grasslands. Rising up slightly you will "T" intersect with Odessa Lake Creek Trail (which at this point is a 2-track as well). This is the end of the line for this trail. If you want a loop, go right on the Odessa Lake Creek Trail, (keep right and stay on main road) which will take you to the main road that the camp is on. Turn right on Lakeview Ranch Road and go back down to camp. For more information, see the Odessa Lake Creek Trail description. One morning the BLM man was mowing the trail from camp to the single tread part of the trail by the first lake. Here he was, in the middle of nowhere on a tractor mowing our trail-what a hoot! He was a helpful guy.

Crater and 3 Lakes Trail, Donna J. & Josie.

Cross Country Shortcut

Distance: 1 Mile approximately	
Altitude: 1595'-1607' about	
Maps: BLM and Washington Road & Recreation Atlas	
Difficulty: Moderate	

Directions: This trail goes into camp on an unmarked area.

Connecting Trail: Odessa Lake Creek Trail

Trail Description: Cross Country Shortcut ride comes off of the north end of Odessa Lake Creek Trail at approximately the ¾ mile-point. There is a small sign reading "No motorized vehicles". Take that overgrown road to the left. (If you miss this turn-off and get as far as a cattle guard, you went too far on Odessa Lake Creek Trail.) Follow the overgrown road which peters out soon. Ride along until you see a small lake. Keep to the left-hand side of the lake and make your way along the grass-laden area to a rocky section above the lake and then down into the dry swamp at the northeast end of the lake. When we crossed the end of the lake, I led my green-broke gelding into the over-your-head grass. If it is wet, I cannot help you make a decision whether to proceed or not. It was dry as a bone when we were there in July. Go uphill on rocky, craggy terrain and presto, you'll see Ranch House Horse Camp down below. Ride cross-county from here on out, heading towards camp. Watch for holes, and of course, rattlesnakes. This ride would be a bit harder to find from camp, but you would just head out and poke around until you find the lake. We used this trail twice, as it is a nice shortcut.

Laurie, Robin, and Wareen cool their feet in water buckets on a hot July afternoon.

Odessa Lake Creek Trail

Distance: 12.5 Miles	
Altitude: 1544'-1609'	
Maps: BLM and Washington Road & Recreation Atlas	
Difficulty: Moderate	

Directions: There are two trailheads for this trail. One is north of Ranch House Horse Camp and the other starts in the town of Odessa. The one in the town I'll call the south trailhead. To reach this trailhead follow the signs in town north of Highway 28. It is only a block or two from the main drag on a short washboard gravel road. There is a large parking area with no facilities. The north trailhead is about ½ mile north of the Ranch House Horse Camp off of Lakeview Ranch Road. There is no good parking and no facilities, just a trail sign. I suggest parking at the horse camp and riding up to the trailhead. Another option is to take the Crater and Three Lakes Trail described in this chapter to reach the Odessa Lake Creek Trail.

Connecting Trails: Cross Country Shortcut, Off Road Vehicle Loop, Crater and Three Lakes

Trail Description: The Odessa Lake Creek Trail runs north and south. Starting at the north trailhead, you'll take an old two-track road from the signed trailhead. Riding west, the trail rolls along a fence line with views of the ranch below. The grasslands and soft footing are easy to make time on. In about ¾ of a mile you'll see a sign down on the left that reads "No motorized vehicles". This is the Cross Country Shortcut Trail. Continue

Jan and Donna E. check out a strange rock pile in canyon.

Laurie & Donna J. ride Odessa Lake Creek Trail.

riding and the next thing you'll encounter is a cattle guard. Go around the cattle guard-the side gate was open when we visited. There was a big irrigation pipe the horses needed to step over. The trail bends to the south and yet another trail leaves. It is just plainly marked "Trail" and this time it goes to the west (right). That is a 2-track and I call it Off Road Vehicle Loop Trail. Keep on going straight and in a short time you will come to an intersection with Crater and Three Lakes Trail. Again the same type of sign-"Trail". That trail leaves, going east (left) down a grassy 2-track. Stay on course, and you'll ride through what was an open fence, slightly uphill. At the next intersection of both 2-track roads, you'll go left. (Everything is marked "Trail", but according to the map this is the original Odessa Lake Creek Trail. Both ways end up together in a short while anyway!) Ride slightly downhill to reach a cool bluff overlooking the Lake Creek Canyon coulée, and what is called the Channeled Scablands of eastern Washington. There is a dry falls here named Delzer Falls. Get out your camera. Next you'll ride along the edge of the rim to the right (south) and see a set of corrals with a fenced-in spring called Waukesha. There is a "Trail" sign here to guide you on. This is about the 3-4 mile point of the trail. From here you will leave the spring, going slightly uphill and will meet with a more main road which veers to the left. Follow this marked trail on two-track road with excellent footing. There is a gate to go through and a sign reading "No motorized vehicles are allowed beyond this point". We found some old farm equipment near here that was fun to photograph. It had dilapidated wooden wheels on it. The next section of trail follows a fence line toward the south and then to the east. The trail drops and becomes a single track with a smattering of rocky footing here and there. Another gate takes you to the canyon below. Here you can go directly down to the valley floor on a cattle trail or choose to stay on the marked trail to the bottom. After reaching the old lake bed you will need to look for

Rock formations in canyon walls

Donna J. and Stitch take a break on ORV Loop

landmarks. One good one on the west side is a pile of flat rocks structured into a circle big enough to stand in, waist deep. Directly across the flat landscape on the east side of the dry lake is another cattle trail. Just follow it and in about 5 minutes, look above for a trail that leads you to water troughs for stock. (A few trail signs must be missing here.) We found two trails that go up this hill to the water tanks-either one is fine to ride. There was cool clean water here for the animals. This is about the half-way mark. On the map, look for Bob's Creek to find this location. From here on, the signs are easy to locate. This portion of the trail is a bit rocky and has a few step-ups. Over-all it is good and not too steep. You will reach the top of the single tread as it "T" intersects with a soft and pleasant two-track road. Follow the trail markers to the south (right). Climb up and roll along on nice tread. The trail parallels the canyon to a series of spring-loaded gates. The Odessa Lake Creek Trail turns to the east, still undulating, and finally goes due south, downhill towards a pole line. You'll see the train tracks and wide open spaces dotted with cattle. Follow a pole line road as it wanders its way east toward the town of Odessa. There is a signed turn-off for the trail going south from the pole line road. Take it to reach the trailhead. It is a single path through the desert. There are lots of small gates to go through. Only one gate was a wire-type and was strung tight. We managed to get it closed and were on our way in no-time. This would be a real nice point-to-point ride, totaling 12.5 miles from town to camp. Part of this trail was hiked by Donna, Jan and myself and part was ridden. We surprised a jack-rabbit from the brush. What a beautiful sight. He was silver-gray and fast as a lightning bolt! Always watch for holes made by the wildlife, and enjoy the plants and beautiful scenery.

Robin and Mojo getting ready to ride.

Rock blind.

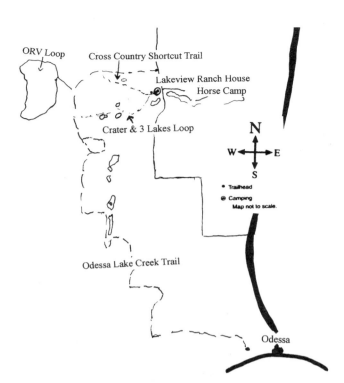

ORV Loop

Cross Country Shortcut Trail

Lakeview Ranch House
Horse Camp

Crater & 3 Lakes Loop

N
W — E
S

• Trailhead
◎ Camping
Map not to scale.

Odessa Lake Creek Trail

Odessa

Josie on Doc, and Wareen on Toby at the canyon rim on Odessa Lake Creek Trail.

Off Road Vehicle Loop

Distance: 4 Miles approximately	
Altitude: 1605' approximately	
Maps: BLM and Washington Road & Recreation Atlas	
Difficulty: Moderate	

Directions: There is no trailhead for this trail. Use the Odessa Lake Creek Trail to gain access. Be sure to include your mileage to and from this loop from camp, for an accurate estimation of riding time.

Connecting Trail: Odessa Lake Creek Trail

Trail Description: Start Off Road Vehicle Loop from Odessa Lake Creek Trail. Ride west on a 2-track road. You'll come to a gate, so be sure to close it again when you enter. You can ride either way from here. The ride is shaped like a lollipop. I'll describe it going to the left. Ride along a fence line for a while to where the Off Road Vehicle Trail veers off to the right as the other trail continues along the fence. Now you are heading north. The trail rolls along and down to a draw. It was beautiful and green here, even in mid summer. We had to stop and enjoy the surroundings for a while. Next you will follow a fence-line uphill to a 3-way intersection. Keep to the right. Follow the 2-track as it bends east and south to come back to the stick part of the lollipop. Trace you hoof prints back the way you came to Odessa Lake Creek Trail. We enjoyed this trek because you can add it on to several different rides to extend your time in the saddle. It is just what a young horse needs.

*Note: I have given most of these trails names. Except for Odessa Lake Creek Trail, I think it will make it easier to differentiate them since they are all marked "Trail". Also be sure that you have permission to wander outside of the BLM boundary. Anything past the Off Road Vehicle Loop to the north and west is either private or "Other" lands.

Water trough on Odessa Lake Creek Trail.

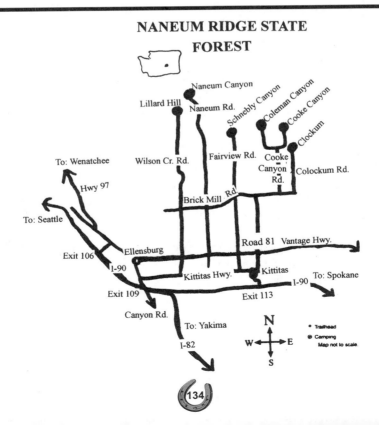

NANEUM RIDGE STATE FOREST

Naneum Canyon

Lillard Hill   Naneum Rd.   Schnebly Canyon   Coleman Canyon   Cooke Canyon

To: Wenatchee   Wilson Cr. Rd.   Fairview Rd.   Cooke   Clockum

Hwy 97   Canyon   Colockum Rd.

To: Seattle   Brick Mill Rd.   Rd.

Road 81   Vantage Hwy.

Exit 106   Ellensburg

I-90   Kittitas Hwy.   Kittitas   To: Spokane

Exit 109   Exit 113   I-90

Canyon Rd.   To: Yakima

I-82

N
W — E
S

• Trailhead
⊙ Camping
Map not to scale.

134

NANEUM RIDGE STATE FOREST

The Naneum Ridge State Forest is located north of Ellensburg, in central Washington. It covers portions of two counties, Kittitas and Chelan. The area is approximately 15 miles by 13 miles and is managed by the Department of Natural Resources (DNR). The Wenatchee National Forest borders this area to the northwest and west. The state forestland stretches north to Wenatchee Mountain and almost to Mission Peak, where you can look down on Mission Ski area. Mixed into the Naneum Ridge State Forest is a checker-board of land run by the Department of Fish and Wildlife. This includes the Aurthur Coffin Game Reserve near Clockum Pass. This is a small area of land about 4 miles by 1-1½ miles and a sort of reprieve set aside for the elk to feed and calve, away from human interference. You will see signs posted and fencing. Also mingled around the edges of the Naneum Ridge State Forest is private owned land. Be respectful of individual property. I highly suggest that everyone have an up-to-date map when visiting this region. There are many canyons, hilltops, old logging roads and meadows to explore. There are no lakes, some seasonal ponds, but loads of streams, creeks and babbling brooks. Bluffs tower above on rocky ridge lines. The views are of the Kittitas Valley. Let your imagination run wild, envisioning how the landscape may have looked to the Indians and explorers. I am highlighting 8 of my favorite spots for trail riding. Be aware of rattlesnakes in the area. They can be quite big. I opted to get my trail dog "Daisy" an annual rattlesnake vaccination shot, which will probably protect her from a timber rattler bite, although nothing is guaranteed. Sheep herds are common in the late spring and summer. The herds are big and noisy. Cattle range here as well. Keep you trail dog under control at all times. Hidden downed-wire and old fencing can be a nasty experience if your horse becomes tangled in it, so always be on the watch and carry a tool on your person for emergency wire snipping. My dad said that "while you are riding near a fence line, be sure to always count the number of strands of barbed wire. If all of a sudden 5 strands become 4, you know a loose wire is underfoot somewhere". So I practice his good advice. There are many gates. Some are the type to keep stock in, and another type of gate is the big metal ones that are locked, (they are shown on the map). These gates are to keep vehicles out and usually there is an easy way around for trail riders. Leave all gates the way you found them. There is room for camping, target shooting, hunting, off road vehicle (ORV) riding, fishing and and most importantly, horse back riding either cross-country or on dirt roads. Whatever your pleasure, I'm sure you'll find it in the Naneum Ridge State Forest. Be sure to clean up after yourselves and leave the area cleaner than you found it. On the back side of the state forest map you'll find written guidelines regarding ORV's, information on green dot roads (GDR), campfire policies, and recreational events. No permits are required to park in the Naneum Ridge State Forest. Be aware of the possibility of logging traffic. Be thoughtful of where you park, especially at the bottom of the Naneum and Cooke Canyons. The school bus needs space to turn around, and there are signs posted "No Parking". There is also access to this area from Wenatchee, although I am not as familiar with that side of the ridge.

For more information contact:

Washington State
Department of Natural Resources
713 Bowers Road
Ellensburg, WA 98926
509.925.8510

Maps to use:
Naneum State Forest- "Green Dot Roads"available from (DNR)
Green Trails Maps (GTM): 243 Colockum Pass
Wenatchee National Forest Map is helpful too

Coleman Canyon Loops

Distance: 9 Mile Loop, or a 12 Mile Loop
Altitude: 2400'-4400'
Maps: GTM 243 Colockum Pass; Naneum Ridge State Forest
Difficulty: Moderate

Directions: *If driving from I-90:* Take Kittitas Exit 115, go through the town of Kittitas and turn right at the "T" intersection on Patrick Road. Drive east (right), on Patrick Road. The road bends around to the north and becomes Number 81 Road. Cross Vantage Highway, still on Number 81 Road.

From Ellensburg: There are two major roads leading east/west from Ellensburg to Road 81: Either drive east on Vantage Highway (in Ellensburg it is named "University Way" then it becomes "Vantage Highway") and turn north (left) onto Number 81 Road. Or you can drive east out of Ellensburg to Kittitas on Mountain View to Road 81. (From Ellensburg this road's name is Mountain View then changes to Kittitas Highway, and when it reaches Kittitas it is called Patrick.) Patrick Road bends around to the north and becomes Number 81 Road. Cross Vantage Highway, still on Number 81 Road.

Any way you come to Road 81, go north. Drive to a "T" intersection then turn right (east) onto Brick Mill Road. Turn left (north) onto Cooke Canyon Road. Again a "T" intersection. This time you will turn left (west) onto a dirt road- this is Coleman Canyon Road. The road winds around, crosses a bridge and goes under some power-lines. Continue on. After you go over a cattle-guard start looking to the left. When you see a couple of trees and a target *Josie and Royal ride up Coleman Canyon.*

practice area, turn in and park. Go slow, the ground is a little on the wavy side. There is another spot to park just beyond this one, at a fork in the road. There is a pull-off and it is big enough for a couple of rigs.

Horse Camping: There is primitive camping spots along the sides of this good gravel road. You can drive all the way in. It is narrow in spots, and creeks are abundant. There is an old orchard and small clearing at the beginning of the canyon. Drive just past a cattle-guard. It is a popular spot for target practice. There is a creek just off to the east down the hill for horse water. Be sure to keep your hay out of reach of cattle.

Trail Description: I'll describe the Coleman Canyon Loops beginning from the parking description above. Ride on the main road north to a "V" in the road where an old road and the newer route are. Ride on the old road. It is to the right (east) and has a berm, so no motorized vehicles can enter. Ride downhill to where the creek is. In a short distance you will notice a spot where the power-lines are, and a small road goes over the creek to the right. Take this little road, ford the creek and head uphill on a pretty rocky area. There is more than one little road at the top that branches off, so stay to the right. You will travel up and through a meadow with a gate and an old logging area. The area is shaped like a bowl. Here you will find a unique water trough. Head up to the crest of the hill and now turn to the left (north) on a small road. This small road leads you to a bigger one. Take the bigger one downhill (east), for a few steps toward Cooke Canyon. At this point you will see Road 8.13.1 going to the north (left) take it. (Don't worry if you don't get all of the turns exactly, as the goal is to get to the top of the ridge that runs north and south between Coleman and Cooke Canyons.) Ride along this ridge (the setting is forestland with nice footing), viewing both canyons at different times. The Lupine flowers in the late spring are beautiful here. This road will take you up and around a deep draw. There is a creek that you can water your horse at when the road takes a sharp westward bound turn. This is about the 4-mile point. The ride levels a bit and there are various roads, but just stick to the main road. Now you are going to go downhill, switchbacking for a couple miles to meet with Coleman Creek Road 8. (You will see the Coleman Creek Road from up on top.) When you reach Coleman Creek Road 8, *turn left if making the shorter loop:* Follow the canyon road all the way back to your rig. You will pass over a metal bridge, see and hear a waterfall way down in a deep gorge, and see lots of camping spots. There will be a side-gate to open at the top of a hill, which avoids the cattle-guard. After the gate you can take the pole-line road or the main road down. Either choice you'll end up at the rig. (I prefer the pole-line as the footing is softer, and you will ride by the creek, where you may offer the horses another drink.) If you stay on the Coleman Creek Road 8 you will ride down to where Dawson Canyon Road 8.4 heads up. Just continue down to the rig. *Now if you choose the longer loop:* Ride to the right (north) on the main Coleman Creek Road 8 going for about 1½ miles. You will see a creek and an old road that has a berm to the left (west) side of the canyon road-take it. (Earlier in the ride from up on Road 8.13.1 you can see this unnumbered road on the far side of the canyon.) Ride or lead over some nasty berms and head up on the only road here. Follow it all the way back as it swings to the south. It parallels Coleman Creek Canyon below. The nice part is, no vehicles are allowed on most of the length of this road, although towards the mouth of the canyon, they are. I like the softer footing on this leg of the ride, rather than Coleman Creek Road 8. It just depends on how long you want to be out too. This little unnumbered road comes out at the mouth of the Coleman Canyon on Dawson Canyon Road 8.4. Go downhill, on Dawson Canyon Road 8.4. It meets up with Coleman Creek Road 8, and you'll ride right back to your rig. In the springtime the longer loop may still be packing some snow. It is shaded and can be prone to drifts, so consider your options. Hopefully you'll see some elk, deer or maybe a black bear on your ride.

Josie and Royal stop at this unique water trough on the ridge between Coleman and Cooke Canyons.

Colockum

Distance: Varies; this area stretches from Ellensburg to Wenatchee	
Altitude: 2800'-5371'	
Maps: GTM 243 Colockum Pass; Naneum Ridge State Forest	
Difficulty: Moderate	

Directions: *If driving from I-90:* Take Kittitas Exit 115, go through the town of Kittitas and turn right at the "T" intersection on Patrick Road. Drive east (right), on Patrick Road. The road bends around to the north and becomes Number 81 Road. Cross Vantage Highway, still on Number 81 Road.

From Ellensburg: There are two major roads leading east/west from Ellensburg to Road 81: Either drive east on Vantage Highway (in Ellensburg it is named "University Way" then it becomes "Vantage Highway") and turn north (left) onto Number 81 Road. Or you can drive east out of Ellensburg to Kittitas on Mountain View to Road 81. (From Ellensburg this road's name is Mountain View then changes to Kittitas Highway, and when it reaches Kittitas it is called Patrick.) Patrick Road bends around to the north and becomes Number 81 Road. Cross Vantage Highway, still on Number 81 Road.

Any way you come, drive north on Road 81. At the "T" intersection turn right (east) onto Brick Mill Road. Turn left (north) onto Colockum Road. Be aware this road is very bumpy and is steep with washboard ridges. Go as far as you like. I suggest you go in a 4-wheel drive vehicle first before deciding whether or not to take your horse trailer up here.

Horse Camping: Roadside only, there are several used camp sites made by hunters.

Trail Description: The Colockum is an extremely rocky area and the road is nasty! It is very popular, despite this negative aspect. There are range cattle up here in the summer and the terrain is mostly open hillsides. The Aurthur Coffin Game Reserve is on top of the plateau-ridge and has lots of cover (trees and brush) for the elk that live here. The drive up here is the worst part, as the riding is okay once you are up. There are a lot of people searching for the coveted big elk antler sheds, so you won't find any lack of company when you visit in the spring. In the fall it is a favorite spot for hunters as well. The road over to Wenatchee is a route that has been used from long ago. Even if you decide not to ride here, it is fun to drive over and down into the Wenatchee valley. It is very steep!

Sue and Willie on a ride during hunting season up Coleman Canyon.

Donna J. and her mare Penny and Josie and her mare Zephyr cool down in the creek.

Paul uses a handy saw called Chainsaw in a Can to cut some downfall from the trail.

Laurie on Rocky, and Donna J. on Penny ride up Naneum Canyon.

Cooke Canyon

Distance: 6 Miles and up	
Altitude: 2800'-5200'	
Maps: GTM 243 Colockum Pass; Naneum Ridge State Forest	
Difficulty: Moderate	

Directions: *If driving from I-90:* Take Kittitas Exit 115, go through the town of Kittitas and turn right at the "T" intersection on Patrick Road. Drive east (right), on Patrick Road. The road bends around to the north and becomes Number 81 Road. Cross Vantage Highway, still on Number 81 Road.

From Ellensburg: There are two major roads leading east/west from Ellensburg to Road 81: Either drive east on Vantage Highway (in Ellensburg it is named "University Way" then it becomes "Vantage Highway") and turn north (left) onto Number 81 Road. Or you can drive east out of Ellensburg to Kittitas on Mountain View to Road 81. (From Ellensburg this road's name is Mountain View then changes to Kittitas Highway, and when it reaches Kittitas it is called Patrick.) Patrick Road bends around to the north and becomes Number 81 Road. Cross Vantage Highway, still on Number 81 Road.

Any way you come, drive Road 81 north. At the "T" intersection turn right (east) onto Brick Mill Road. Turn north (left) onto Cooke Canyon Road. Again a "T" intersection. This time you will turn right (east). This is still Cooke Canyon Road. Continue on past some houses and the school bus turnaround. The road becomes gravel and narrows as you enter the canyon further. I like to park down underneath the pole line on a small road to the right. There is a creek here as well. There is enough parking for several small rigs. You may also drive further and park off the main road in the shade of pine trees, with the babbling creek nearby.

Horse Camping: There is primitive camping spots along the sides of this good gravel road.

Trail Description: Cooke Canyon Road 8.13.4 takes you about 6 miles, then you can climb up towards Colockum Pass on smaller roads, and ride as far as you want going cross country. The main canyon road becomes more steep at the end of this box canyon. I have ridden on most of the side roads. A nice ride is to go west under the pole line on Road 8.31.1 riding up to the ridge between Cooke and Coleman Canyons for scenic views. As always, be on the lookout for fence-line rubble. I have seen wild turkeys and lots of deer, elk and other miscellaneous wildlife in this cozy canyon.

Paul and Midnite enjoy a late fall ride near Ellensburg.

Paul and Midnite take 5 up a local canyon.

Sandy & Chris find an elk antler to bring home.

Dawson Canyon

Distance: 4 Miles	
Altitude: 3300'-4400'	
Maps: GTM 243 Colockum Pass; Naneum Ridge State Forest	
Difficulty: Moderate	

Directions: Use the same directions as for Coleman Canyon. Dawson Canyon is reached by riding up Coleman Canyon about 1 mile from the orchard parking area.

Horse Camping: I have none to suggest in this narrow little canyon, although you may be able to. I would camp down in Coleman at the orchard/shooting area.

Trail Description: Dawson Canyon is used to make loops in the area. Starting from the orchard/shooting area go up Coleman Creek Road 8 for about 1 mile to a fork in the road to Dawson Canyon Road 8.4, which is marked. (Not the small power line road. You'll use that if you make a loop-see below). Coleman Creek Road leaves, going right. The Dawson Canyon Road is cool and shady in the late day and has rocks-however they lay so flat in places that it is more like a cobble stone path. Which can be slick when it is wet. In about 3 miles, Schnebly Canyon joins in. Continuing on this road, the names change, according to the newest map. (Naneum Ridge State Forest) Dawson Canyon becomes Beavert Road but maintains the same number which is 8.4. If you want, you can follow the road to where the 4-corners intersection is. (If you are going to the Naneum Canyon Road 7.11 you can take Boulder Creek Road down to Walter Flat.) *For a Dawson Canyon loop:* You could go back down on the Schnebly Canyon Road. It goes over a small pass then down to the springs. From here, head east on an unnumbered road by the power line and it will bring you back to the intersection of Coleman Creek Road and Dawson Canyon. It makes a nice 8-9 mile ride and a loop! Consider making a point-to-point ride starting at Cooke Canyon, over to Coleman, then over to Schnebly Canyon, (or even Naneum Canyon). The possibility is there.

Naneum Canyon- High Creek

Distance: Varied	
Altitude: 3600'-4950'	
Maps: Naneum Ridge State Forest; GTM 243 Colockum Pass	
Difficulty: Moderate	

Directions: Leaving Walter Flat at the 7 mile-point.

Horse Camping: If you're packing-in you may or may not be able to camp at Walter Flat. It is closed sometimes due to over-use, so call ahead to plan your trip. Otherwise you can find a spot along the road/trail.

Trail Description: From Walter Flat (described in the Naneum Basin Ride) you will take Naneum Basin Road back down the canyon for about 1½ miles, then turn right (west) up the High Creek Road. Follow this road and go explore. You can ride it up to where High Creek runs under a little bridge, (which is about 3-4 miles from Walter Flat) then travel up some more to a level plateau. Wander around and go back down using the same route or travel cross country down a steep draw near the mouth of the canyon (experienced rider & horses only). You can also ride some other roads that branch off High Creek Road to come out above Walter Flat. There are two ponds just west of Walter Flat, shown on the Green Trails Map. They are seasonal, so in case you are using them for a landmark, they may only be small meadows in the late summer and fall. There are views of the whole Naneum Valley

Laurie says to always leave the gate as you find it. She took a turn opening this one for the rest of us.

from the High Creek Area. The roads are nondescript and conditions depend on the time of year and severity of run-off down the roads.

Naneum Canyon-Naneum Basin

Distance: 7 Miles	
Altitude: 2400'-3600'	
Maps: Naneum Ridge State Forest; GTM 243 Colockum Pass	
Difficulty: Moderate	

Directions: From Ellensburg, drive east on Vantage Highway to Naneum Road. (In Ellensburg, Vantage Highway is named University Way then it becomes Vantage Highway outside of town.) Turn north (left) onto Naneum Road. Drive about 8.5 miles on paved road to its end at a big gravel area. This parking area is used by the school bus for a turnaround, so don't block the gravel parking area. I suggest to turn around, then drive back as far as you can, keeping to the side of the road to leave maximum space for the bus. Naneum Road is a dead end. There is a locked gate to the entrance of the canyon, and parking is not permitted past the bridge, and private driveway.

Horse Camping: You can pack-in. This is a locked gate canyon with no camping at the trailhead.

Trail Description: To begin the Naneum Ride, ride from the parking area going west, cross the bridge still on pavement, and straight ahead you'll see the big metal gate across Naneum Basin Road. There is a trail around the gate on the right hand side. *To ride the creek valley:* Horseshoeing back toward the river, go along the fence to a small hand-gate. Open, go through, and shut it behind you. Riding the valley bottom, you will follow the path, crossing the creek twice. There is a bridge for the first one, although I do not trust it. It is **very old** so I ford the river on both crossings. There is a wire gate. Be sure to leave it the way you find it. The meadows along the valley are big and have nice footing. In a mile or so you'll come out on Naneum Basin Road. T*o ride Naneum Basin Road;* Go to the left after going around the big metal gate, and back up onto the gravel road to begin this ride. You'll ride uphill and then back down. Open and shut a side gate to avoid the cattle-guard. In about 1 mile you'll meet up with the creek valley path as the road levels at the bottom of the hill. I use the road in the spring to avoid two, deep swift-water crossings. Believe me, you do not want to chance getting swept away in high waters! Follow Naneum Basin

Road for a ways, using cattle paths when you want to. They run alongside the road. As always, watch for wire. There is a cattle-guard with a side gate on the left. Ride Naneum Basin Road for a short while, then you'll spot the beginnings of a big meadow with a wetland area running through it. Follow the path that takes you down across the wet spot. Continue gently down a little more and around a knoll on an old logging road. Go through a wet, rocky area near the creek, (but not over the creek). You may have to duck under some small limbs in here. Always watch for wire. The trail goes further around the knoll, then travels uphill quite steeply to reach a small road. Go downhill on this road (to the right) and cross a nice sturdy metal bridge with the option to ford the stream. Follow this old road along the creek's east bank (resist temptation to go off on spur roads, they dead-end anyway). It is pretty easy to follow here, and the road rises with nice views of the river valley. The footing is great. One spot that some people get lost at is a corner that becomes very rocky. It is tempting to go on the lower road, which does seem like it coincides with where the path has been going, but this time go on the rocky one, uphill. Ride over some berms, leading you east to a rock slide area. The trail switches direction again, going north, down along the edge of the rock slide to cross Boulder Creek. Be aware, this may be tricky for a green horse or horses that don't do water crossings well. It has some mud and is a narrow spot with overhanging branches and brush. The creek is not very big and not deep. Your horse won't sink but he doesn't know that. Ride steeply uphill, and when you're almost at the top, turn to the left. Go over a small berm and head downhill. Follow this old road along as it winds around a seasonal pond and over rocky areas and small streams of water here and there, with views of the river basin. When you reach the end of this ride you are at Walter Flat. It is unmistakable-set in tall timber with an old camp area. Here several roads come together including Naneum Basin Road that leads to where you parked down below. You can ride Naneum Basin Road back if you want. However, there can be logging-truck traffic and the road is pretty hard packed. There is another big metal gate on the road back. I have always been able to go up and around it. Usually Sundays are non-truck days. Be aware that there can be loads of livestock in this canyon in the grazing months. This includes cattle, and massive herds of sheep along with the sheep herder's mobile trailer and his pack of 5 plus dogs, which may come running out to you if they are around. The trail is not marked like a Forest Service trail, so just remember to stay on the main paths and roads when in doubt.

Naneum Canyon-Swift Creek

Distance: Varied	
Altitude: 3600'-6742'	
Maps: Naneum Ridge State Forest; GTM 243 Colockum Pass	
Difficulty: Moderate	

Directions: Leaving Walter Flat , see Naneum Basin Ride

Horse Camping: If you're packing-in, you may or may not be able to camp at Walter Flat. It is closed sometimes due to over-use, so call ahead to plan your trip. Otherwise you can find a spot along the road/trail.

Trail Description: Riding from Walter Flat, follow the Naneum Basin Road north. It quickly branches. Go to the right up Swift Creek Road 9.13. Here you'll be able to cut cross country. As the road winds around you can cut off some mileage by cutting the corners. There once was a cabin about 2 miles up from Walter Flat. We used to go there and have lunch, a fire, and sometimes even stayed the night. The cabin had a sign-in book and people had wonderful stories to tell. The cabin was on the boundary line of Chelan and Kittitas County and as long as nobody wrecked it, or it became a mess, they were willing to leave it standing, because neither county claimed it as their own. Unfortunately someone rammed their vehicle into the side of it and it was demolished after that. Using your map to guide you to Wenatchee Mountain, take Road 8 up to Naneum Ridge Road 9 and go west. This is a 4-wheel drive road and is kind of rough. If you ride to the lookout site at Wenatchee Mountain and Mission Peak you will pat yourselves on the back for making the enormous effort to trek up here. On the way up you will pass a meadow that is named in honor of one of the Rodeo City's Grandmas. For those of you who don't know them, they are legendary cowgirls that lived and ranched in Ellensburg. They had stayed together and were in parades and I even got to move cows with one once. Boy could she ride! She drove one of those old horse-vans. Out she came and away she went, quick as lightning. Anyway, these areas were some of their favorite spots and were named in their honor. You can see over Naneum Ridge to the ski runs at Mission Ridge Ski Resort. Looking south you'll see the entire Naneum Valley, clean down to the Kittitas Valley. It is breathtakingly beautiful. I hope it is a clear day for you.

Schnebly Canyon

Distance: 5 Miles	
Altitude: 2400'-3600'	
Maps: Naneum Ridge State Forest; GTM 243 Colockum Pass	
Difficulty: Moderate	

Directions: From Ellensburg, drive east on Vantage Highway to Fairview Road. (In Ellensburg, Vantage Highway is named University Way then it becomes Vantage Highway outside of town.) Turn north (left) onto Fairview Road. Follow this road about 5-6 miles and when the road takes a 90 degree corner to the left (which is where it becomes Thomas Road), Schnebly Canyon will be straight ahead through the gate. Drive in about 1 mile. Go over a cattle-guard to a large open spot on the right and park. Always shut the gate!

Sue and Willie stop for a while.

Josie on Royal watch some cattle up Schnebly Canyon.

Horse Camping: There are lots of spots to camp in this canyon, just look for a wide area. There is a stream that runs alongside the road for the first couple of miles, although the first mile or so is "off limits" as it is private land. After that you can park and camp.

Trail Description: Ride Schnebly Canyon Road up into the canyon. It is quite rocky. You'll pass a stream, go through a gate around the cattle-guard, and see another parking area. From here you'll follow the road as it climbs to the trees, with Schnebly Creek along the side of the road. I have seen lots of elk and deer and I know people who have seen cougar as well. There is a cool spring at a flat area and a big parking area, which is a

Jackie and Vanilla at Walter Flat in the Naneum.

popular spot to camp from here you can go several directions to make loops. But for now we will continue on the Schnebly Canyon Road. There is a chance that one more gate will be shut, so if it is, make sure to close it after you go through. Cattle are caught by surprise grazing, lounging and chewing their cud. They are everywhere in the summer! The canyon goes up, flattens out, and then up some more. It raises up to its high-point then descends down to meet with Dawson Canyon Road 8.4 at a "T" intersection. You can make a lot of loops in this area, most of which have better footing than the main canyon road. Watch for downed wire and have fun.

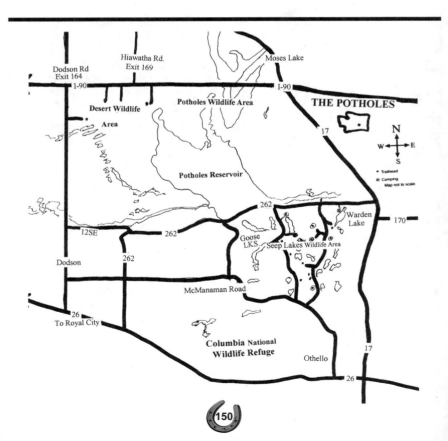

POTHOLES RECREATION AREA

Potholes Recreation Area is situated in Washington. Moses Lake is the closest big town on the northern border and Othello is to the south. All of the present lakes are a result of irrigation water, due to the rising water table from the construction of Grand Coulée Dam in 1934. The Columbia National Wildlife Refuge was established in 1944 and actively managed since 1955. I rode this with several friends and we had a lot of fun exploring the different areas. It is best to split this region into three portions. Each part has its own characteristics. The southern half is called "Seep Lakes Wildlife Area", the northern fragment-"Potholes Wildlife Area", and the eastern part-"Harris Desert Wildlife Area". This coincides with the Potholes Recreation Area map. Each section has its own access and would need to be driven to separately. The terrain varies from spot to spot. It is a smörgåsbord of dry sandy desert with mule deer romping about, to swamplands, sloughs, canals, and streams. Lakes are filled to the brim with fish, and different birds are plentiful. You'll find rocky outcroppings with tall bluffs overlooking waterways, razor sharp edged rocks, and soft meadows. The wetlands smell earthy and sweet, and are teeming with life. Other wildlife include several types of ducks, and coots-which are mistaken for ducks. Besides waterfowl, look in the basalt cliffs for hawks, owls, swallows, Great Blue Herons, Sandhill Crane and ravens. Some make their homes here and others migrate through. You may also see coyotes, muskrats, and beaver living in the area. Bobcats and badger are seen occasionally. Some of the "Seep Lakes Area" has cattle grazing upon it. I love the way-out-west feel. Endurance rides have been held here, and I'm sure the area was selected for the expanse of open range terrain. There are at least 60 lakes in the Potholes Recreation Area, not counting the massive Potholes Reservoir. If you fish, or if your riding friends do, there are a host of choices of fish to catch. The same goes for bird watching. In the fall, some spots are open for hunting. The riding is moderate in difficulty. Signs posted indicate that horse riders are welcome to ride on the same roads that are open to vehicles. The chance for an encounter with a Western Rattlesnake exists, so be aware, especially around rocky areas and heavy vegetation. We saw only non-venomous snakes when we visited. There is a state park at the edge of the Potholes Reservoir. It is not meant for equestrian use. The park is green, shady, and spacious. It is a nice place for a family picnic. There are a few hiking trails to the west of the park. Conveniently located in the hub of the activity is Potholes General

Store. There is gas and diesel available as well as a restaurant. You'll find it on the opposite side of the park, just off Highway 262-O'Sullivan Dam Road. It is on the south side of the road. This is where I found some useful maps. You will need a parking pass called WDFW "Vehicle Use Permit". If you have a current fishing license, you will already have the pass. There will be a fine of at least $60.00 if caught without the pass. I hope you will visit this part of Washington State, for it offers yet one more place to ride, especially in the off-season. In the meantime, the snow can melt off the hills in the spring, and collect on the ridges in the fall. And we can Ride, Ride, Ride!

For more information contact:

Refuge Manager
Columbia National Wildlife Refuge
735 East Main Street
P.O. Drawer F
Othello, WA 99344
509.488.2668

Maps to use:
Washington Road & Recreation Atlas
Potholes Recreation Area
Columbia National Wildlife Refuge Washington

Eastern-Harris Desert Wildlife Area

Distance: 14 Miles approximately	
Altitude: 1050' approximately	
Maps: Washington Road & Recreation Atlas; Potholes Recreation Area; Columbia National Wildlife Refuge Washington	
Difficulty: Moderate	

Directions: To drive to the eastern fragment of the Potholes Area called "Harris Desert Wildlife Area", you will take I-90 to Exit 164, which is just east of the town of Moses Lake (Dodson Road). Go to the south and take the Frontage Road, maybe 1 mile back toward Moses Lake left (east). Turn south (right) onto a road that has a little brown and white sign that reads: "Public Fishing-Public Hunting". Drive this small sandy road as it winds around with several spots to park. One loops around, coming to

Donna E. scans the area on a foggy autumn morning.

Cheryl & Sophie say to pack out all of your garbage.

Donna J. and Penny with her tongue sticking out at the camera.

the end at a sandy turnaround. We went to the end and turned around and backtracked to a roadside spot so if another rig came in there would be room for them to get turned around as well.

Trail Description: Donna E. and I rode this section of the Potholes in November and had a nice ride. From the parking area you can see a lake. There is a 2-track road here which you can follow for a ways before it peters out. We made a 4½ hour loop going cross country and as we stumbled upon the little road on our way back, we saw several bird hunters and heard the far off shots. The sand is quite deep and the horses got a good work-out. There is less sand and more stable footing the closer you stay to the lake edges, of course without going into the swamplands. Be sure to watch for downed fencing. Use a "soft eye" on the horizon for fence posts-this will alert you to possible wire hazards. We did find a gate to go through. Be sure to always close the gate if it was closed when you found it. We lunched under a nice plot of Russian Olive trees that had deep green grass for our horses to munch on. When we arrived, it was so foggy we could hardly see 50 feet, then when it lifted we saw the beautiful steamy landscape. The desert has its own magic and the surrounding farmland with the winter wheat just sprouting up was breathtakingly beautiful. Be glad you live in the U.S.A. and come and enjoy this land. We were able to get the horses a drink near where we parked at the lake.

Josie tends to the geldings in the Russian Olive grove.

Northern-Potholes Wildlife Area

Distance: 9-10 Miles approximately

Altitude: 1050' approximately

Maps: Washington Road & Recreation Atlas; Potholes Recreation Area; Columbia National Wildlife Refuge Washington

Difficulty: Moderate

Directions: To drive to the northern piece of the Potholes Area simply called "Potholes Wildlife Area", you will take I-90 to Exit 169, which is just east of the town of Moses Lake (Hiawatha Road). Go to the south and take the Frontage Road 2.5 miles back toward Moses Lake left (east). Turn south (right) onto a road that has a little brown and white sign that reads: "Public Fishing". There is a smaller blue sign that reads Road 5501-however I'm not sure what it means. The way it is angled it could either be for the Frontage Road or for the Public Fishing Road. This is a dirt road. It is rolling and has some washboards, so go slow . You'll go over a filled-in cattle-guard. There are hay fields on one side and desert on the other. You are driving next to power poles. All roads will dead-end at parking areas with lakes. I'll describe the roads in the order that you come to them while driving. At the first "Y" intersection, you'll follow the power-line to the left (east). Then quickly veering left again at the second "Y" will lead you to a vandalized vault toilet and parking area. This is a short road. Now back at the second "Y", but this time staying to the right, is a longer road that is rolling. It leads to a camping area with an awkward turnaround near a power pole. Both of these roads go toward the green wet areas and they are very nice to visit. From the main road at the first "Y" we will go right. Drive until you see another split. One road goes downhill and one stays up. If you choose the one that stays up, you'll find great views of multi lakes and waterways. It is a fairly long road and it dead-ends at a wide open spot on a bluff. It looks like a target practicing area. If, instead, you choose to go downhill (right) at the split, you'll find my favorite parking area, which has nice new gravel and a clean vault toilet. There is plenty of room to turn around for any size rig and parking for at least 4 rigs. It is about 4.5 miles from the paved road for this parking. This area gives you access to the best riding too. See the map for more clarity.

Trail Description: My friend Donna J. and I visited this area in July and found it to be surprisingly beautiful. It is the prettiest of all the spots, I think. We parked at the farthest west parking area where there is a nice gravel parking spot and a vault toilet. We rode west and into some deeply treed areas where the big white Sandhill Cranes, Great Blue Herons and black raven were, next to the lakes. We wandered out to where no unauthorized vehicles are allowed and rode along a nice 2-track for about 4-5 miles until it dead-ended near the frontage road. We passed wetlands and desert areas. It was quite interesting. We were lucky that it never got too hot. After we got back, we went to several other lakes which were a couple miles in the other directions from where we parked. I would tell you the names, but they are not on the maps that I have. There are plenty of water holes for the horses.

Birds enjoy the summer day in one of the many lakes.

Donna J. and Penny.

Southern-Seep Lakes Wildlife Area

(Morgan Lakes Road)

Distance: 9-10 Miles approximately	
Altitude: 1050' approximately	
Maps: Washington Road & Recreation Atlas; Potholes Recreation Area; Columbia National Wildlife Refuge Washington	
Difficulty: Moderate	

Directions: The southern half of the Potholes Area, referred to as Southern "Seep Lakes", has a few choices to park. It has two parallel roads leading into the Seep Lakes. The east road is called Seep Lakes Road, the west road is called Morgan Lakes Road. You will need to drive to either Road 12 (closer to Othello) on the south end or Highway 262-O'Sullivan Dam Road (closer to Moses Lake) on the north end. The eastern and western entrances are about 1-2 miles apart. See the map for more information. For the Morgan Lakes Road riding area, I like to park at a gravel spot at the intersection for Upper Goose Lake and Morgan Lakes Roads. There is a vault toilet and a fair sized opening for several rigs. The other nice spot is by Soda Lake near the boat launch, but don't block it. You can back into a big parking area with a hill behind you, and the lake beside you. The Morgan Lakes Road is an easier gravel road for rigs, but either one works. Every place has rules-here they are: Dogs must be on a leash, (except hunting dogs when being used) swimming is prohibited, and littering is unlawful. Take your trash home with you. All firearms are prohibited except shotguns which are okay in public hunting areas during hunting season. Horseback riding is allowed on gravel roads open to vehicle use. Park in designated areas 1 hour before legal sunrise until 1 hour after sunset. Camping and overnight parking is permitted in Soda Lake Campground only. Fires are allowed only in a camp stove. No removing of or searching for objects of antiquity. No dirt bikes, three and four-wheeled ATVs, or snowmobiles are allowed on the refuge. Fishing is offered in over 50 lakes and sloughs. There are 15 miles of streams and canals open during portions of the year. Hunting ducks, geese, pheasants, and others is permitted in marked "Public Hunting Area" only. We noticed several small roads were marked closed October 1st through March 1st.

Trail Description: My friend Donna J. and I rode this leg of the Seep

Lakes in the early summer. We had a nice ride and were able to visit many lakes. We started at a parking area located by the intersection to Upper Goose Lake. It has a gravel pullout and a vault toilet. We rode uphill to see Upper Goose Lake, where you can look down into the hole that the lake sits in. We saw a big snake-thank goodness it was only a bull snake. We then rode back and had lunch at the rig. There is a trail here, but it is hiker only. Next we explored these lakes; Soda, Migraine, Dadwall, and several others that were just "Potholes". We followed what looked like the canal for a long ways. We certainly got a taste of the area and were pleased with our find. This makes a great place to ride, especially when the snow is on the mountains. We drove all around and saw the rest of the lakes and then exited toward Othello. Water for the horses is not a problem in this area.

LOCKED IN THE ARMY RANGE

One cold December day I decided to go for a ride on the John Wayne Trail down by the Columbia River in Washington. I went alone on my mare "Ali". I entered the road and gate on the Army range that leads to the trailhead parking. Sometimes the gate is closed and sometimes open. It was open this day and I was delighted. I drove the 2 miles of one-lane sandy road to the trailhead, parked and rode for only a couple of hours. (It had been getting down to below zero at night and I needed to get home in a timely fashion. The sun goes down so early at this time of year, I knew a short ride was in order.) When I returned to my truck I noticed a note under my windshield wiper. It read: "Combination to John Wayne Trail lock" and gave the numbers. (I'll leave out that information.) I figured it was the combination to the gate that I had driven through at the entrance to the Army land. I loaded up my mare and drove back the 2 miles on the one-lane sandy road, got out and dialed the combination. What happened? It didn't work! Maybe I did it wrong, so I did it again. Nope! I uttered ##!!@@...and a few other choice words. The John Wayne Trail runs parallel to this road, although you are not able to access it due to deep sand, rocks and uneven ground. The sun would be down in an hour or so, so I needed to make a decision fast. I could either ride my horse to the nearby town of Vantage, (which is about 3 miles away on paved road) to call for help from the gas station, or I could back my trailer the 2 miles to the trailhead and drive down the John Wayne Trail and out the trail-gate. Before I made up my mind, I walked over to the trail-gate and dialed the combination to make sure it worked. It opened right up. I started backing my trailer up. I'd need to be careful to stay on the road since the sand on either side was deep. It is way harder to back up for miles than you would ever imagine. I did about 1 mile of serpentine, snake-like tracks before I found a spot that I could, inch-by-inch, turn my rig around. Thank God I only have a two-horse trailer! I drove the other mile pretty quickly. I held my breath as I drove down the slim trail. My heart pounded as I crossed the old trestles, hoping they would hold the weight of my rig. I folded my mirrors in on my truck narrowly slipping my rig between a couple of huge cement blocks to get through to the gate. Just in time, considering the sky had turned that beautiful rose pink and red after the sun has sunk in the far west. By this time the temperature was in the single digits and getting colder. I felt blessed to have gotten out in such a timely manner. Sometimes I get the feeling someone up there has a lot of laughs at the goings-on here on earth. I will leave a note next time I go off alone, so someone will have a clue where I have gone.

Southern-Seep Lakes Wildlife Area

(Seep Lakes Road)

Distance: 4-5 Miles approximately	
Altitude: 1050' approximately	
Maps: Washington Road & Recreation Atlas; Potholes Recreation Area; Columbia National Wildlife Refuge Washington	
Difficulty: Moderate	

Directions: The southern half of the Potholes Area, referred to as Southern "Seep Lakes", has a few choices to park. It has two parallel roads leading into the Seep Lakes. The east road is called Seep Lakes Road, the west road is called Morgan Lakes Road. You will need to drive to either Road 12 (closer to Othello) on the south end or Highway 262-O'Sullivan Dam Road (closer to Moses Lake) on the north end. The eastern and western entrances are about 1-2 miles apart. See the map for more information. For the Seep Lakes Road you can park easily near Long and Sage Lakes. There are graveled areas and vault toilets. I would recommend staying out of Marco Polo Lake parking as it is tight. My friend Sue and I did it once. That is before we knew the area. Each of these 2 main roads (Morgan and Seep Lakes) are about 10 miles in length. The Seep Lakes Road has several washboards, especially on the northern end. Every place has rules-here they are: Dogs must be on a leash, (except hunting dogs when being used) swimming is prohibited, and littering is unlawful. Take your trash home with you. All firearms are prohibited except shotguns which are okay in public hunting areas during hunting season. Horseback riding is allowed on gravel roads open to vehicle use. Park in designated areas 1 hour before legal sunrise until 1 hour after sunset. Camping and overnight parking is permitted in Soda Lake

Donna J. at one of the beautiful lakes.

Road in to the Seep Lakes area.

Campground only. Fires are allowed only in a camp stove. No removing of or searching for objects of antiquity. No dirt bikes, three and four-wheeled ATVs, or snowmobiles are allowed on the refuge. Fishing is offered in over 50 lakes and sloughs. There are 15 miles of streams and canals open during portions of the year. Hunting ducks, geese, pheasants, and others is okay in marked "Public Hunting Area" only. We noticed several small roads were marked closed October 1st through March 1st.

Trail Description: My friend Sue and I visited this area in mid December and although it was a short ride I felt as though we got a lay of the land. We rode to these Lakes: Marco Polo, Susan Lake, Katy, and then to the overlook of Sage Lake. We rode down into the valley holding these lakes: Sage, Upper and Lower Hampton, and Long. Then it began to sleet (mix of rain and snow) which pelted our faces and stung. The sky grew very dark so we backtracked to the rig. There are no trees or places to escape the weather. We had fun,

but to get better pictures of the area I returned on a nicer day. This leg of the Seep Lakes is more arid and has rolling hills. The other leg off of Morgan Lakes Road is more mini-canyon lands. The footing was nice and sandy for our ride. Watch for cattle. We drove out towards Othello on that end of the road. We noticed the deep canal with the cool metal bridge over it. We saw more lakes than we could remember. There have been endurance rides held here. We were able to get the horses drinks as there are many lakes.

View of the canal from the metal bridge.

Rustic signs.

Lakes are everywhere for you to enjoy.

CODY HORSE CAMP

Cody Horse Camp is located in south central Washington State. This is a newer horse camp and may not be on all maps. It is nestled on the west side of Mount Adams. This camp is within riding distance of a much bigger and well known horse camp called Keenes Horse Camp. (The detailed information on Keenes Horse Camp can be found in my last book "Trail Busters".) My husband Cliff and I visited in October and the colors were just starting to change. There was snow on the upper sections of trails. You can view the beautiful Mount Adams from some of the trails. The only trail to leave the horse camp is Klickitat Loop #7A. It is a 27 mile trail. My husband and I hiked up from Cody Horse Camp, and other parts were ridden to from Keenes Horse Camp. I've also included a few connecting trails that my friends Sandy, Terri, Madeleine, and I have ridden, to give you a feel for this area. Maybe you will ride some of the trails that I didn't and can someday tell me about your adventures on them. This area is in the Gifford Pinchot National Forest, which is one of the oldest National Forests in the United States. There are at least 1,200 miles of trails in this National Forest. Over 13 rivers in this area are being recommended to be added to the national "Wild and Scenic Rivers System". The White Salmon River is already enjoying this prestigious title. Edible berries include huckleberries (higher altitudes) and blackberries (lower elevation). Some of the Sawtooth Huckleberry Fields are reserved for local tribe members only. This was brought on by the Great Depression when jobs were scarce and berry-picking was over-done. There was an agreement between the Forest Service and the Indians to reserve certain areas. My husband Cliff and I found lots of palatable fall mushrooms. We followed bear and deer tracks on the trail. Other wildlife that are found in the area are elk, cougar,

View of beautiful Mount Adams from Klickitat trail.

Sandy crosses Muddy River near Keenes Horse Camp.

and mountain goats. There is small game like grouse, bobcat, coyote, fox, raccoon, and rabbits, along with a large variety of other woodland animals, fish and birds. There is an informative sign at near-by Orr Creek Sno-Park. It shows a map of the surrounding mountains, indicating dates in which the timber harvest began and when it was replanted. Other products are also harvested from this National Forest. They include: cones from the trees, evergreen boughs, transplant trees, Christmas trees, beargrass, salal (shrub or bush), firewood, and common minerals. Always check with the local Forest Service before removing anything from the Gifford Pinchot National Forest. Take home good memories and "Leave No Trace".

Directions to Cody Horse Camp: *Coming in from the north:* From Highway 12 near Randle, turn south onto Road 25-131 for 1 mile. Veer to the left on paved Road 23 for 18 miles. Turn left again on Road 21 for about 5 miles. From this point it is about 9 miles more to camp. Turn right onto gravel Road 56 for about 3 miles. Here the sign reads "Horse Camp 10 miles". This road begins as paved and becomes gravel. At the next intersection the sign reads "Keenes 8 miles"and "Cody Camp 2 miles". (The landmark is Orr Creek Sno-park.) Keep straight, still on Road 56. (You would turn right and go past the sno-park if you were going to Keenes.) Follow the road to the signed turnoff to Cody Camp on Road 5600-059. In ½ mile on good road you are at the loop and camp. *Coming in from the south:* Begin by driving on Highway 14 along the Columbia River to Road 141. Go north for 25 miles. You'll go through the town of White Salmon to another town called Trout Lake. At Trout Lake, by the gas station, turn north (right) onto Mount Adams Road. In 1 mile, Road 23 leaves to the left. Take it and drive

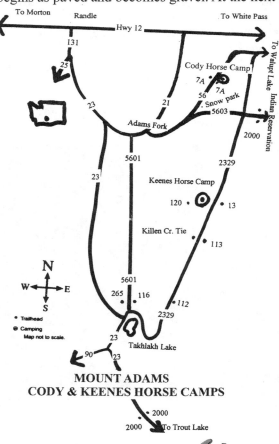

MOUNT ADAMS
CODY & KEENES HORSE CAMPS

on until you see Road 2329. It goes towards Takhlakh Lake. Go past the lake and continue driving. Drive 6-7 miles. You will pass Keenes Horse Camp. Go 2 miles further to an intersection and turn left on Road 5603-go downhill to Orr Creek Sno-park. At this intersection, (which is signed, "Cody Camp 2 miles") you will need to go right on Road 56 for 2 miles. Follow the road to the signed turnoff to Cody Camp on Road 5600-059. In ½ mile on good road you are at the loop and camp.

Cody Horse Camp includes: Cody Camp is a nice new camp with 16 drive-through campsites and has cable high-lines that have rings to tie to. There are tables, a vault toilet, fire pits, and cement manure bins. There is a water system that is unique. You first pump the water at a separate location in the center of camp by the green gated lane. The water then goes through a pipe and comes out at a water trough, which is downhill from the pump. This is potable water and stock water as well. Camp is free. There is a day-parking area that is quite large and has a mounting ramp. In the day-use area is also the trailhead for Klickitat Trail #7A. I like this camp. A lot of times the horse camps are on a slant, but this one is well thought out and any slight slope is hardly noticeable. Be a good neighbor and observe quiet times and run generators between 6 A.M. And 10 P.M. only.

For more information contact:

Cowlitz Valley Ranger District
10024 US Highway 12
P.O. Box 670
Randle, WA 98377
360.497.1100
www.fs.fed.us/gpnf/

Maps to use:
Gifford Pinchot National Forest
Mount Adams Wilderness
Green Trails Maps: 334 Blue Lake
　　　　　　　　　366 Mt. Adams West
　　　　　　　　　367S Mount Adams
CowboyMaps.com: Mt. Adams Keenes Horse Camp

High Lakes #116

Distance: 7.7 Miles

Altitude: 3800'-4400'

Maps: GTM 334 Blue Lake; Mount Adams Wilderness; Gifford Pinchot National Forest

Difficulty: Moderate

Directions: From Cody Horse Camp ride Klickitat Loop Trail #7A for 1.9 miles. High Lakes Trail #116 leaves to the right (south). Be sure to add this mileage into your ride.

Connecting Trails: 7A, 120, 120A, 115, and 265

Horse Camping: Keenes Horse Camp or Cody Horse Camp

Trail Description: Starting from the intersection with Klickitat Loop #7A and High Lakes Trail #116. You are only ½ mile from Midway Meadows. The area is open to motorcycles since this trail is outside the Wilderness boundary. You head south on High Lakes Trail #116 and cross paved Road 5603. The path is forested and cool. You will ford Muddy Creek which is not deep and the banks are not muddy. However, the water is muddled, hence the name Muddy Creek. You will meet Keenes Trail #120, #120 A (No Name), and Spring Creek Trail #115. As you near Horseshoe Lake you'll notice a spur trail. Keep to the main trail and go around the lake in deep woodlands. The trail is more strenuous as you continue along. You will ford Killen Creek. Descend in forest where you'll find two creeks. One is clear and one is glacial water with the milky color to it. Adams Creek has a nice long bridge across it, which is equipped with side rails. This trail travels by a lava flow and then over it. You ascend and cross the lava out of a narrow steep canyon. It is amazing how well-placed the trail is. The trail goes by a small lake on the left-hand side, which is part of the Chain-Of-Lakes. Next is a parking area and a meadow. Go past this and down to road 5601 where the trail ends. This would be a long trek from Cody Camp, so for all those hard-core riders, this ride is for you!

Keenes #120

Distance: .6 Mile

Altitude: 4361'-4300'

Maps: GTM 367S Mount Adams; Mount Adams Wilderness; Gifford Pinchot National Forest

Difficulty: Moderate

Directions: This trail connects High Lakes Trail #116 and Keenes Horse Camp

Connecting Trail: 116

Horse Camping: Keenes Horse Camp or Cody Horse Camp

Trail Description: This is a short .6 mile long trail. It is all in forest. I included it so you can link up the trails from Cody Horse Camp to Keenes Horse Camp. It goes along Spring Creek and has a few bridges. It will tie-in to the lower of the two camp loops that make up Keenes Horse Camp, coming out near the water tank. A lot of trails are near by.

Bri rides Prince on a nice summer day.

Sandy on Chris and Josie on Ali have fun on the trail.

Klickitat Loop #7A

(#7A Cody Camp to Trail #7B)

Distance: 6 ½ -7 Miles

Altitude: 3000'-4600'

Maps: GTM: 334 Blue Lake; Mount Adams Wilderness; Gifford Pinchot National Forest; CowboyMaps.com: Mt. Adams Keenes Horse Camp

Difficulty: Moderate

Directions: This trail begins from Cody Horse Camp

Connecting Trails: 7B, 115A, and 116

Horse Camping: Keenes Horse Camp or Cody Horse Camp

Trail Description: I will describe this trail starting from the day use area at Cody Horse Camp. Klickitat Loop Trail #7A goes steady uphill ending at Trail #7B. This trail is a loop and extends for 27 miles. However, I can only tell you about 7 miles of it. Begin in old growth forest headed east. The trail goes across a seasonal wet area on a bridge. Climbing up, my husband Cliff and I saw some bear tracks. There are long switchbacks, and some hillside trail, which is well placed and wide. In about 1 mile or so you'll cross an old overgrown road. Next you will be traveling parallel to a bigger dirt road. It is above you. Soon you'll come up to it and see a destination sign that signifies: Trail #7A-straight ahead across the road. Klickitat Loop #7A can also be reached in 2 miles to the east via Trail #7B. It was a bit confusing until I realized that Trail #7B at this point is this road. Go uphill to some level spots. It is steeper here than below the road. You'll ride next to a deep ravine and up some more to the top. Here it becomes level. Ride down slightly through lots of bear grass, where it is more arid. Now a bit of hillside traveling with a drop-off area. It is short-lived and the trail is good. In fact, the view of Mount Adams is very nice from this spot. Next is an intersection with Trail #115A. The destination sign reads: Trail #115 2½ miles. (Trail #115A looks pretty rugged.) Continue on to Midway Meadows. The trail goes up and up some more for the next .5 mile with nice footing in forest. You will come to a road with a sign "7A Klickitat". Turn to the left here. This trail becomes a road for a short while, passing through Midway Meadows. High Lakes Trail #116 leaves going south. In a short while the trail becomes a single tread again on the right hand side of the road. In about 1 mile the trail will come to a major road-Road 2329. Cross over the dirt road kitty-corner, via the bridge. Here there is a cute cabin with a stove in it and a spot to water your stock in Midway Creek. The elevation is 4490'. We saw some fall mushrooms as well as motorcycle tracks on this trail. Go uphill and then level out a bit. The trail travels through nice forest and meadows. In about 2 ½ miles to 3 miles you will see Trail #7B. This is as far as I have gotten on this loop.

Ski hut and primitive camp site along the #7A Trail.

Sandy & Chris, Josie & Ali at the Pacific Crest Trail near Keenes and Cody Horse Camps.

Cliff, (Josie's husband) and trail dog Tess hike part of the trail from Cody Horse Camp.

Trail marker guides you on the Klickitat Trail.

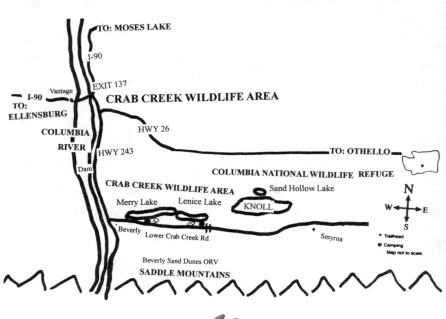

Lower Crab Creek Road is located in Central Washington near the Columbia River and the town of Beverly. Part of these trails are in the Crab Creek Wildlife Area and some are in the Columbia National Wildlife Refuge. This is a great place to ride in the spring and again in the late fall. In the summer it would be too hot for most people. It is a desert area with sagebrush and tall bushes. There is an abundance of Russian Olive trees that are pretty, but do have thorns on them. There are lots of choices for riding. You can go see the blue sparkling lakes, the wavy eerie sand dunes, and the unforgettable Milwaukee Road Corridor, which seems to run endlessly as it parallels Lower Crab Creek Road. There is also a power line road that comes in handy to make loops. The footing is generally soft and sandy for the horses. You can camp down along side of the road in spots. Be self sufficient and pack out all trash. As a general rule, sand dune lovers with their ORV's (Off Road Vehicles) keep to the south side of Lower Crab Creek Road and fishermen and horseback riders keep to the north side of the road. Always be watchful for rattle snakes. In the early fall when they are shedding they may not rattle before striking. No fees or special permit signs were posted whenever I have visited.

Directions to Lower Crab Creek: Drive on I-90 to the Columbia River near Vantage. Take Exit 137 going south on Highway 26 toward Othello. Then after about ½ mile leave Highway 26, and continue south on Highway 243. Follow the Columbia River just past Wanapum Dam and the town of Beverly. Watch for Lower Crab Creek Road. Turn left (east) on Lower Crab Creek Road. The trailheads are described below for each ride listed.

Camping includes: Primitive camping along Lower crab Creek Road.

Map to use: Washington Road & Recreation Atlas

Merry and Lenice Lakes Loop

Distance:	8-9 Miles
Altitude:	500'
Map:	Washington Road & Recreation Atlas
Difficulty:	Moderate

Directions: Use the above directions to reach Lower Crab Creek Road. Drive east (I like to set my truck's mileage trip meter at "0".) When you reach the 1.9 mile-point on paved Lower Crab Creek Road, turn left onto a small gravel road where the sign reads: "Public fishing". The trailhead is at the end of the road.. There is enough space to turn your rig around by the vault toilet, as well as a separate spot which is long and narrow and is easy to back into.

Trail Description: Ride across the Milwaukee Road Corridor to a fence line, and stay on the right-hand side of the fence on a well beaten path, following it to the northeast. When the lakes are in sight, you may follow any number of paths to the shorelines. Be prepared for deep, soft, sandy areas. Go toward the east along the lakes. Here you will need to watch your horse-my green-broke gelding thought it would be a nice spot to roll. He never even stopped-he just went down. If this happens don't panic. I kept my head and gently nudged him until he regained his footing and then urged him onward. Even seasoned horses may try this in the deep sand. Let them know this is not on the menu today. There are some small boats stored along the shoreline that are on a permanent anchor under lock and key. They are turned belly-up and may surprise your horse. There are lots

Josie, Doc, and Daisy above Merry & Lenice Lakes.

Donna E. and her gelding Andi ride by Lenice lake.

of trees, tall brush, and maybe a fisherman lurking quietly, fishing for his dinner. Merry Lake and Lenice Lakes are so close to each other that you may not notice when one ends and the other begins. Follow the path as it takes you up and alongside some tall rock outcroppings (watch for wire and stay on the main trail). Here you can follow numerous game trails. Just motor-along above the lake area on a ridge, or dip back down towards the lakes again. Eventually you will come up to the ridge area. Cross a small road coming out of the lakes, and continue east cross-country. Soon there is another major road coming from the lake area. Here you'll turn onto it, to the right (south) toward the Saddle Mountains. The road becomes gravel here. You will see a parking area and a vault toilet. This is where you will catch the Milwaukee Road Corridor. Go to the right (west) on it back to your rig. This is a leisurely ride and takes about 3 hours if you are not in a hurry.

Josie and Chief at an old homestead along the Milwaukee Corridor, Saddle Mountains in the backdrop.

Bridge over Crab Creek on the Milwaukee Corridor, trail dogs Tess and Daisy come along too.

Milwaukee Road Corridor

Distance: 13.5 Miles	
Altitude: 500'	
Map: Washington Road & Recreation Atlas	
Difficulty: Moderate	

Directions: Coming in from the west by the Columbia River, go east. Set your truck's mileage meter at "0" and when you reach the 1.9 mile-point on paved Lower Crab Creek Road turn left onto a small gravel road to the trailhead. The sign reads: "Public fishing". There is a turn-around by the vault toilet and also a long narrow parking area for backing into. Milwaukee Road Corridor goes in two directions. Another spot to park that is less popular is at the 11.7 mile-point on Lower Crab Creek Road. You'll do a "U" turn onto a dark gray gravel road. Drive to a wide turnaround. The trail is right there. Ride between some rocks and a hill to access. Watch for wire. The trail goes east and west from here as well.

Trail Description: From the first trailhead listed above, the Milwaukee Road Corridor goes to the west for only 1.9 miles reaching a housing area and is pretty nondescript. Going to the east, it travels along, straight-as-an-arrow for 11.6 miles. It will take you along the old rail grade with sprawling views of the towering Saddle Mountain Range to the south and bluffs to the north. It is pretty quiet except for the occasional fishermen traveling into the lakes, or a far-off buzz of 4-wheelers on the sand dunes. Everyone gets to enjoy their piece of the recreation pie down here. You'll ride over trestles and alongside marshy areas, tall wild grasses and willows where birds may be nestled-in, giving flight periodically. I like this area because the elevation is low, which makes for less snow and ice, and open winters are not uncommon. It dries out and greens up early in the spring. If you like practicing riding faster, or are working with a young or inexperienced horse letting other horses advance and retreat around you honing their skills, this is a great place to do that. There are interesting old structures here and there alongside the trail. You'll cross 2 trestles-one is long and goes over Crab Creek. We noticed missing pieces of wood on the longer bridge, so be careful if you decide to cross these trestles. Be aware that the ground may be quite swampy next to the old rail grade. If you get away from the beaten path, even if the ground surface doesn't appear wet, you may be in for a surprise. In places there is wire from old fence-lines. Some of it is hidden down underneath the dirt and grass, so if you get off the railway, be careful where you tread. I always carry a multi-use tool that has a pliers with a wire-cutting edge on it just in case. When you reach a paved road and a small community, you are at the 13.5 mile-point and from here on it is sketchy. The corridor continues a bit more, although this is where we turned around. I think that it peters out soon anyway. Another rail system comes alongside within a mile or so. If you like feeling as though you are in the middle of nowhere, you will like this ride.

Crab Creek and Saddle Mountains at Christmas, view from the Milwaukee Corridor.

This is the view of the knoll from Milwaukee Corridor that has Sand Hollow Lake tucked behind it.

Sue on Willie and her husband Paul on their mare Dusty at Sand Hollow Lake.

This is the gate you will go through from the Milwaukee Corridor to begin Sand Hollow Lake Loop.

Josie and Harley on Sand Hollow Loop Ride.

Bridge on Milwaukee Road Corridor.

Sand Hollow Lake Loop

Distance: 10 Miles approximately	
Altitude: 500'	
Map: Washington Road & Recreation Atlas	
Difficulty: Moderate	

Directions: Driving on Lower Crab Creek Road going east, you will go on paved road for 3.1 miles. Keep going on good gravel road to the 6 mile-point. Park on the wide shoulder of the road or go a tad bit further, cross a bridge, and there is a circle parking area just beyond. You can access the Milwaukee Road Corridor from here. You will go east (right) on it to start your ride.

Trail Description: To start Sand Hollow Lake Loop you will go down the Milwaukee Road Corridor to the right (east) for several miles. When you reach a big gate on the left, go through it and head north on an old two-track road that intermittently becomes a path. You'll come to a power line road. Turn right (east) and follow this for several miles to a main dirt road. It climbs up and over a big ridge, then drops down to beautiful Sand Hollow Lake. Ride the south shore-line on a well defined path. This is a good spot to have some lunch. Our goal here is to go around a knoll that is on your left side toward the south. As you continue riding, go west beyond the lake. You'll see an old homestead to the north. There is a gully and a swampy area. Don't cross the ravine, but instead keep yourselves on the skirt of the knoll. Go around the end of the knoll. It requires a little cross-country, but just remember your landmarks, and head south toward the Saddle Mountains. The Milwaukee Road Corridor is straight ahead. Cross it and you'll be back to the rig. The power line was the only section that was a bit rocky. Be aware that hairy, hot horses may try to roll in the deep sand. Overall, this ride is quite a workout for the animals because of the soft footing. We enjoyed it with the late autumn sun feeling wonderful on our faces and backs as we shuffled along in the silence of the sandy footing. We will be back soon.

COAL MINES TRAIL

The Coal Mines Trail is located in central Washington. It links up the towns of Cle Elum, Roslyn, and Ronald. It is a multi-use trail that sticks to the abandoned Burlington Northern Railroad bed. These towns had coal mines in and around them and the main object of the Coal Mines Trail is to utilize this area as a recreational corridor. There are several ways to access the trail since it crosses many roads and goes through several towns. You can do all or part of the path depending on your mood. I like to ride it in the spring especially, because it is not muddy, and it is level making it an easy ride which is perfect for when the horses are just getting conditioned. Also, the snow melts off here earlier than in the mountains. In the fall it is nice to ride because the leaves are turning, making a beautifully colored ride. You can ride to the end and have lunch at Old No. 9 restaurant/bar, which has a tie-rail to tether your horse to, or you can stop off and have a latte' from the Roslyn Cafe (and lunch as well) while enjoying the old mining memorabilia outside the restaurant. Coal Mines Trail offers a chance for your horse to be ridden next to and encounter things not usually seen on a mountain trail, such as a playground, and a park with people and strollers. There was construction going on one fall with hammering and big equipment moving dirt around. You will cross several paved roads, so be careful. You may want to dismount depending on the time of year and day, and whether the traffic is heavy or light. In the fall also, you can escape the hunters and shooting as there is none allowed on this trail. There are usually hikers, joggers, fellow riders, and/or bike riders on the trail, which is welcome activity if you are sacking out your horse to everything you can think of. Next to the trail at about the ½ way mark there is a stream off to the side of the trail. It has a gravel road running smack-dab in the center of it and the edges of the water-crossing are perfect for training the non-seasoned horse to cross water. I used this several times on my little dun horse "Doc" and it was perfect. I think Coal Mines Trail is a great place to stop if you are traveling. It is close to I-90 and you could exercise your horse's legs if you are on a long haul.

Direction to Coal Mines Trail:
In Cle Elum, the trailhead is at the west edge of town. First Street is the main road through town. Turn north off of First Street onto Stafford Avenue (a good landmark is a stop light, American flag, and the Chamber of Commerce log building). Go to the next corner, which is Second Street

West. Cross this intersection and you will see the trailhead. The parking is roadside only. There is a portable toilet here and a trail sign. In Roslyn, you can park as well. Drive through town on the main street, which is First Street, then turn right onto Dakota Street where you will see the parking area among the old gray slag piles. The trail is on the north side of the parking area.

For more information contact:
Cle Elum Chamber of Commerce for a small booklet

Map to use:
There is a map posted in several spots along the trail, so you really can't get lost on this trek. A map is available at the Chamber of Commerce. It is called "A visitor's guide & map to Cle Elum, Roslyn, and upper Kittitas County".

COAL MINES TRAIL

Coal Mines Trail

Distance: 4.7 Miles
Altitude: 1922'-2375'
Map: There are maps posted along the trail
Difficulty: Moderate

Trail Description: Starting on the Coal Mines Trail from Cle Elum you will travel westward for 4.7 miles to its end at the town of Ronald. Riding behind some houses, it can be somewhat busy near the trail as people, horses and dogs live here. Go across a small cement depression in the trail, made for drainage. You will notice that benches have been put along the trail for people to sit on. There are nice informational signs telling the history of the trail. The trail goes from Cle Elum, through the town of Roslyn, then ends at Ronald. You will cross several paved roads, so be watchful for traffic. There is a spot to water your mount about ½ way down the trail on the left-hand side. You will ride a variation of land, from quiet country scenery to smack-dab in the center of town in Roslyn. At Roslyn you will be crossing the main drag-First Street and E. Washington Avenue. Ride on about 3 blocks of pavement lined with businesses and residential housing. The trail resumes at the park. Kind of like being in a parade! (Follow the white stripes on the pavement that are made to look like a railroad track.) One block to the south (left) of the park, is the Roslyn Cafe', (famous from the T.V. hit show Northern Exposure) where you can get lunch and a latte'. We partake of them almost every time we ride the Cole Mines Trail. Donna J. and I like to enjoy our treat and look at the old mining relics by the cafe'. Continue on to the park where there is a restroom, as well as a map-board showing where you are and points of interest along the trail. The trail continues on behind the park in cool forest. Now you will ride to the outskirts of Roslyn and on into countryside again, cross another road and travel the fringe of the next town, Ronald. There is another main paved road to cross, more sitting benches, and a small road to go over near the end of the trail. The trail ends abruptly. (Use this road to head downhill to town, turn right on the main road in town and go to the Old No. 9 to eat and drink, or simply turn around.)

I've included some history of the area: This trail was dedicated to the hearty pioneers that settled here. The Coal Mines Trail was formed by Kittitas County, the City of Cle Elum and the City of Roslyn in 1994. Coal was mined from 400' below Cle Elum to the top of the ridge to the north.

You will notice remnants of the mining operation left behind. It is dumped into piles called slag heaps. No. 7 dump burned for many years when it caught fire from spontaneous combustion. The leftovers were red shale which is an ingredient in making cinder blocks. This dump was closed in 1937. Another place along the trek is "Happy Hollow". It may have been named for the tranquil surroundings. Settlers leased land from Northwest Improvement Company (NWI) and raised food and livestock. A spot named "Coal Washer" is where they washed the coal, graded it, and sized it into categories: pea, nut, and egg. Left behind is an estimated 3 million tons of washer-waste dump. "Mine Camp No. 5" housed a settlement of Eastern European immigrants on 20 acres. There were 32 4-room houses. The area children followed the coal trains, gathering miscellaneous coal pieces that spilled from the train cars and would tote their coal-laden gunny sacks back home. The families used the coal for heating and cooking. At the "Mine Workings" at mine No. 5 there were several structures, as well as a tipple. This was a device that emptied the mine coal cars by tipping them to the hoppers which then filled the train cars. This site closed in 1948. Spur Line to No. 9 is about 1 mile and it connected No. 9 rail to the main rail line for moving coal and supplies. It closed in 1963 and was the last working mine to close in the Roslyn coal field. Close to mine No. 4 is "Ducktown" named for the fowl that was raised and used to feed the "Slavic" speaking neighborhood in Roslyn. No. 4 mine was a deep vertical shaft, (626') with tunnels that went horizontally under the city. On Oct. 3, 1909, 10 men were killed in an explosion at No. 4 mine. They felt an impact like an earthquake, and every building within 200', plus the tipple was obliterated. It happened on a non-working day, otherwise there could have been up to 400 lives at risk.

Donna J. and Penny examine the map.

There was a place called the "Shaft Street Power House" which was made of brick and was powered by a coal-fired steam boiler. The need for working mine mules ended when modern electricity came along in 1926. Near the power plant was a privately owned foundry, that opened in 1921, which supplied the Forest Service with metal works. Next on the list is a spot called "NWI Co. Horse Barn" which was a wooden-sided stable used to house the hard working mine livestock. Horses worked topside and mules below ground. In 1892 the horses helped load a 50,000 pound lump of coal onto the rail to be shipped by rail-line to the "Chicago Worlds Fair". There were 26 saloons in Roslyn and they used horses to deliver the beer from the brewery. The No. 1 Mine had the first coal to be shipped by the railroad in 1886. It also had the biggest disaster in the history of Roslyn. In May of 1892, 45 miners died. They theorize that it was from inadequate ventilation, and mine gases may have ignited from the open flame of the lamps, which were used by the miners. There is a site which had a warehouse, wash house, garage, and machine shop. These were all important to the miners for baths, repairs and parts for company rigs. This site was burned by the Roslyn Fire Department in 1965. There were mining offices in town that handled sales, and mining operations. Coal bills and power bills were paid here as well. Engineering offices were also needed and were located here. So too were the mine officials' residences. The "Roslyn Depot" was the train depot, and was next to the NWI Company Store. Passengers and freight were handled here. In 1916 the town became snowbound. Nothing moved-not mail, not supplies. There was 7' of snow! That year they had 21' 8"! Wow, that was some year! The "NWI Company Store" held food, clothes, tools, furniture etc.., for the miners to supply themselves with. They would have the sale costs deducted from their checks. The famous song with the words: "I owe my soul to the company store" sure fits here. The store was open from 1886-1957. "Runje Field" is a park that was a school athletic field and a playground. In 1950 the Old-timers Picnic had 1,500-2,000 people attend. Some of the activities they played at the park included: clay pigeon shoot, bocci ball, and races. Some of the races were sack, obstacle, bicycle, 3-legged, foot, and

Josie & Harley stop for a latte' at the Roslyn Cafe.

(my favorite) fat-women's race. The "Powder House" was made of local sandstone. It was used to house the blasting powder, and later used as cool storage for dynamite-hundreds of tons of it! It was located as far away as possible from residential areas, due to the danger from explosions. The term "Brassing" comes from the brass tokens issued to the miners for buying powder. The company could keep tabs on usage and the names of the buyers. Mine No. 3 "Tipple" was directly above the rail line. It closed in 1957, but was once the longest, continuously operating coal mine in Washington. No. 3 "Cole Mine Dump" is located behind Ronald. There are slag piles, which burned for years, causing a red color. An explosion in 1928 under Falcon Hall caused the loss of 32 homes in Ronald and burned 80 acres. It was caused by a 250 gallon still that had blown up. When the mules were retired after long hard years in the mines, they were put out to pasture in an area called "Mule Pasture". They blindfolded the mules when they reached the surface of the mine. It prevented them from going blind from the light after all the time spent underground, which for some was the majority of their lives. Electric motors replaced the mules in the mid 1920's. Roslyn had a population of 4,000 plus in the 1920's which is 4 times the population number today. Cle Elum had 3,200 people, which is double today's population. Cle Elum means "Swift water" in the

Daisy, the trail dog at one year old, figured out how to stay cool on a trail ride.

Yakima language. In the heyday of mining, the class photo from Roslyn Elementary had children from 24 different nationalities or ethnic groups. What better way to learn a little history than to ride, look, and read! Ride the Coal Mines Trail. If you stop in Roslyn at the Roslyn Cafe' be sure to visit the old coal mine relics around the building. There is a museum that is a small building with a glass front which has old equipment in it, a regular museum, a small coal train filled with coal, and a small building with a "Mucker" out in front of it. This is a machine used to clear and load rock from the mine. I hope you will enjoy this area.

JUNGLE/RYE CREEK LOOP

BY DONNA EVANS

Jungle/Rye Creek Loop

Distance: 10-12 Miles approximately	
Altitude: 2800-4000'	
Maps: GTM 209 Mount Stuart Wenatchee National Forest	
Difficulty: Moderate	

Directions: This trail is in the Teanaway Area in central Washington. Drive I-90 to the town of Cle Elum. Go east on Highway 970 to Teanaway River Road. Drive north on this road for 13 miles-it is all paved. When you reach 29 Pines Campground the road becomes gravel. Park here. There is a small pull-out which is right before where the road changes from paved to gravel. Roadside parking only and room is limited.

JUNGLE/RYE CREEK LOOP
TEANAWAY

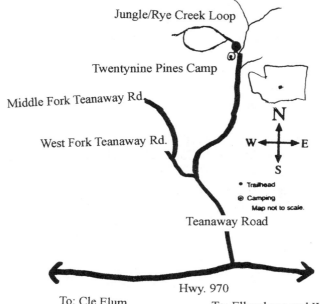

Jungle/Rye Creek Loop

Twentynine Pines Camp

Middle Fork Teanaway Rd.

West Fork Teanaway Rd.

N

W ← → E

S

• Trailhead
◎ Camping
Map not to scale.

Teanaway Road

Hwy. 970

To: Cle Elum

To: Ellensburg and Wenatechee

Connecting Trails: 1383A and 1235

Horse Camping: There is a horse camp named Indian Camp on the Middle Fork Teanaway Road, primitive camping on the Stafford Creek Road, and DeRoux Horse Camp at the end of the Teanaway River Road, but no real campground here for horses. If the road directly across from this parking area is not gated, you could possibly find a primitive spot, although I would suggest driving up without your rig and checking it out first.

Trail Description: This loop is about 10-12 miles long. It consists of mountain Road 9701, currently in use, a short section of trail, and an old mountain road that has been closed off to vehicle use. The ride starts from the end of the county road where we parked. The first four miles or so are ridden on a gravel road that sees little vehicle use. It follows the drainage on a gradual climb up through the forest. About 2 miles along, Jungle Creek Trail #1383A takes off to the north. In about another 1.5 miles, Way Creek Trail #1235 intersects with the Jungle Creek Road. This is where the road veers sharply to the left (south) and ends in an area called "Liars Meadow". The forest opens up and the path travels through a meadow for about ¼ mile where it then turns into a good trail. The trail follows the contours of the hillside and soon climbs steeply up a short section to reach the top of the ridge. The ridge top opens into an old logged off clearing. Here the trail ends and the ridge follows an old logging road down some mild switchbacks, coming to an intersection of four roads. Follow the first road to the immediate left. This is about two thirds of the way along the Rye Creek Road which travels between the North Fork Teanaway, and Middle Fork Teanaway drainages. Follow the old jeep road, which is actually more like a wide cow path. In fact when my husband, Dean and I rode this, there were cattle about halfway down this drainage browsing in some beautiful meadows. The road meanders through lush foliage and eventually travels alongside small Camp Lake. Of all of the fall rides I have been on, this was by far the most colorful. The road continues on down to a gated bridge. Just before the bridge, jog to the left and down a small path to the creek. Cross over and ride back onto the Jungle Creek Road where the ride started.

Josie and Ali near Jungle/Rye Creek Loop.

Mountain goats. A momma and her kid.

BEEZLEY HILLS

Beezley Hills are located on the west side of the town of Ephrata in eastern Washington. This area offers nice springtime riding when the snow is still too deep to go to the mountains to play. The grass is lush and the hills provide a great way to condition your horse for the upcoming riding season. The footing is rock-free for the most part. There is no established horse camping, so my friends and I have always chosen to day ride. It would make an excellent place to stop and stretch your horse if you were traveling across the state. Ephrata has lots of nice places to eat as well. You can put on some mileage in this area. There is opportunity, too, for a wide range of ways to ride. You can either ride cross-country, or follow some roads that criss-cross all over. There are springs, but just in case, I would suggest that you bring some water in your rig for your horse. If you're looking for a simple ride and don't have time or energy to travel off the paved roads, this may be a great playground for you.

BEEZLEY HILLS

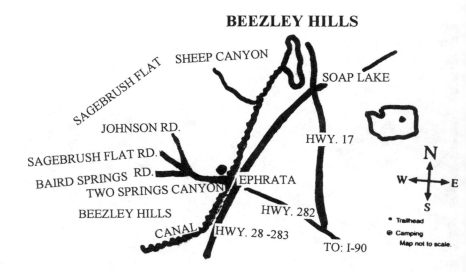

Beezley Hills

Distance: Varies
Altitude: 1250'-2882'
Map: Washington Road and Recreation Atlas
Difficulty: Moderate

Directions: From I-90 take Dodson Road Exit 164. Go north to the town of Ephrata. Dodson Road merges with Highway 28 at town. Or take several other highways from I-90 north to Ephrata: either Highway 17 to 282, (which comes out of Moses Lake) or you can drive Highway 283 near George, Washington. Highway 283 also merges and becomes Highway 28 at town. When you get to the town of Ephrata, you'll turn east onto Street Canal Road (19th Street). Go uphill, across the bridge over the canal, to a wide spot and turnaround and park. There is room for several rigs.

Trail Description: Starting from the parking area you'll head uphill. You have the choice of riding the dirt roads or taking the side paths, which have probably been made by cattle. Be sure to leave all gates the way you find them. There are open hillsides with grass and flowers in the spring. Once you are on top of Beezley Hills you'll find views of the surroundings. To the far west is Moses Coulée, to the north by Sagebrush Flat is housing, and to the southwest is Lynch Coulée. If you go down to the south, there is a somewhat steep gully. If you go down there you will end up at the

This bull elk just lost his antlers. Notice the circles on his head.

Quincy Lateral Canal. The same canal winds around to the north and to the east and is then called West Canal. The canal itself has a no trespassing sign, but we found that there is a paralleling trail/old road that will bring you back to the rig from the north. One time a friend and I went up Two Springs Canyon to Johnson Road and made our way north, to come back down Sheep Canyon Road, (which is a pretty big road), then rode back next to the canal for a nice loop.

Bye for now.
Always remember to
ride, ride, ride your horse . . .
gently down the trail.

INDEX
(Trails listed by name)

HORSE CAMPING INDEX

INDEX

(Trails listed by number)